DATE DUE

Prentice-Hall Series in Automatic Computation

George Forsythe, editor

Critical Factors
in Data Management

PRENTICE-HALL INTERNATIONAL, INC., *London*
PRENTICE-HALL OF AUSTRALIA, PTY. LTD., *Sydney*
PRENTICE-HALL OF CANADA, LTD., *Toronto*
PRENTICE-HALL OF INDIA PRIVATE LTD., *New Delhi*
PRENTICE-HALL OF JAPAN, INC., *Tokyo*

Critical Factors
in Data Management

Edited by
FRED GRUENBERGER

Informatics Inc.
Sherman Oaks, California

Prentice-Hall, Inc., *Englewood Cliffs, N. J.*

Current printing (last digit):

10 9 8 7 6 5 4 3 2 1

13–193540–2

Library of Congress Catalog Card Number 74–81315

Printed in the United States of America

Foreword

The symposium on Critical Factors in Data Management/1968, jointly sponsored by Informatics Inc. and the University of California at Los Angeles, was the fifth such public forum on topics of current interest in the field of information processing. Topics in this continuing series have been as follows: 1964, Disk Files; 1965, On-Line Computing Systems; 1966, Computer Graphics; 1967, Computers and Communications—Toward a Computer Utility.

The 1968 symposium was held in Schoenberg Hall on the UCLA campus March 20–22 and was attended by nearly 400 representatives of industry, government, and education.

It is obvious that a public forum of this size cannot be staged without extensive planning and preparation. The joining together of the facilities and planning expertise of the UCLA Engineering and Physical Sciences Extension staff with the skills and interest of the Senior Staff members of Informatics has provided an outstanding example of the benefits gained when education and industry work together.

FRED GRUENBERGER

Preface

Simultaneously with the introduction of third generation equipment, data processing was forced to direct its attention to a series of maturing problems that demanded immediate action. In addition to the normal demands of accuracy and speed in arithmetic calculations that had sparked earlier developments in hardware, new problems were at hand. Operating systems were available that placed the emphasis on throughput instead of the speed of an individual calculation. To the operating system was added the function of supervisory programs working in a multiprogramming environment. On the basis of this, on-line systems were proposed for a variety of applications. Now computer system analysts had to be communications experts to cope with the problems introduced by terminals, transmission lines, and unique software problems.

From the viewpoint of the analyst, the solutions to problems associated with the management of large data files and data bases had progressed substantially, but the bewildering variety of data usage posed by new applications raised problems of organization, means of file manipulation, storage, and retrieval. Data bases were growing, were used in new ways, and interacted with other data bases such that the best capabilities of previous computers, storage, and communications equipment began to appear inadequate.

In another of the fortuitous coincidences of history, there appeared to be an ideal match between third generation hardware and problems awaiting solution. Intricate plans were made for solving the problems with new equipment working with improved efficiency and reliability. Now, years after the introduction of the new equipment, the promises are not fulfilled. New solutions have been proposed, new companies have been formed to meet the challenge, but with all, there is a growing feeling of cynicism.

This symposium was organized to look clearly at the "critical factors" in data management. Why had the development of large systems fallen behind schedule? What were the causes? What are the implications? What are the lessons that can be learned from the years of trying?

The common thread in organizing the symposium reported in these proceedings was the problems associated with the management of large data bases on the new computing systems of the third generation. Leaders in developing data management techniques were asked to discuss the achievements and future needs for cost-effective data management—in terms of hardware, software, and system design. The intended purpose was to concentrate on the role of data management tools in a variety of applications—in commerce, industry, and government. These applications are the ones raised by the constant growth of information deemed critical to the conduct of government and business and by the pervasiveness of automation techniques. In some instances they require reference to many decentralized data bases in the system that, in turn, raises problems in the compatibility of data structures and communications, as well as the protection of privacy. Attention is paid to the steps that are being taken to provide generalized techniques, permitting broader scope for file usage and application.

ROBERT W. RECTOR
Informatics Inc.
Sherman Oaks, California

Contents

Critical Factors
in Data Management

Critical Factors in Data Management

FOSTER H. SHERWOOD

Vice Chancellor, University of California, Los Angeles

It is my pleasant task to extend, on behalf of UCLA, our welcome to this distinguished gathering. In so doing, I cannot help but remark on the cosmic nature and importance of the tasks you have set for yourselves in this three-day symposium. Indeed, the tasks that grow out of the nature of your subject matter are reflective of some of the most exciting and prescient tendencies in modern life. Certainly, one in my position can claim no special insight or right further to define or delimit your inquiry. Nonetheless, as a layman to your concerns, I think it worth noting that we have passed the shakedown phase of large computer development.

Accordingly, now it becomes incumbent upon all of us, expert and non-expert alike, to deal with the question of purpose in data management in ways that perhaps have not heretofore been used. Such questions as the level of service to be provided, the relative importance of convenience and of speed, ready approximation versus final accuracy of results are questions that arise with increasing urgency.

But beyond these questions lies, I believe, a major shift in user philosophy and user psychology. Until very recently most users approached the problem of data management somewhat cautiously, to be sure, but primarily from the point of view of determining what new and better ways there were for accomplishing tasks that had already been set and were being accomplished in other less efficient ways. Now, however, our users represent a generation raised not to think in these terms but rather to ask the question: "What can I now do that could never have been attempted before?" Thus the system and its equipment becomes the inspiration, rather than the servant, of a program, and a whole new series of problems and challenges are thus created. I suggest that these will serve as a focus of your attention. In pursuit of answers to these questions you have our best wishes and hopes.

Time-Sharing Systems: Analytical Methods*

LEONARD KLEINROCK

Associate Professor of Engineering
University of California, Los Angeles

1. INTRODUCTION

As data bases grow and as the number of users requiring access to the data grows, so grows the rate of conflict among these users for access to the computational power that manipulates and modifies the information contained in data warehouses. This competition for simultaneous use of resources is resolved principally by use of time-shared computer systems. It is imperative that we understand the behavior of time-shared systems well enough to be able to predict their performance in a variety of situations. This is accomplished through the use of mathematical modeling and analysis which, in the last 5 years, has begun to take place. The results of some of these investigations will be reported in this chapter.

2. DESCRIPTION AND DEFINITIONS

A time-shared computer system may be viewed as a set of processors, memories, and terminals all interconnected by a network of communication channels. Superimposed upon this set of hardware resources is a population of users, a set of shared programs, and a set of programmed scheduling algorithms that order the assignment of resources to user requests as they are serviced in the system.

When service is effected according to an a priori scheduling algorithm, the communication network is used to gather user requests arising at

*This work was supported by the Advanced Research Projects Agency (SD-184).

3

unscheduled times and to distribute results after servicing ordered queues of requests. Each job is generally taken to completion in this batch servicing mode. When service is effected according to a dynamic scheduling algorithm, then processing time quanta, which may be variable, are assigned to each request. When more than one quantum is needed to satisfy a request, a system of queues is used to automatically establish relative queue position based on priorities, quantum requirements, and time in-queue. The total processing time required for each request is a variable quantity called *service time.* Processor capability and storage occupancy are variable properties determined by the user requests and the assignment and sequencing algorithms incorporated in the service facility. Priorities arriving with user requests can affect both the position in-queue and the assignment of resources.

We now consider the scheduling algorithms in a little more detail. A *scheduling algorithm* is a set of decision rules determining which user will next be serviced and how long he will be given use of processing and storage facilities. Thus a newly entering request is placed in a system of queues and, when the scheduling algorithm decides, is given a turn in the processing facility. This turn may or may not be sufficient to satisfy the request. If sufficient, the request leaves the system; if not, it re-enters the system of queues, leaving a partially completed program and partially processed data in storage, and waits until the scheduling algorithm decides to give it a second turn, etc.

When a request is given a turn in the processing facility, two other generally dependent scheduling algorithms come into play. One assigns and sequences processors to the request; the second assigns and sequences storage space in the storage hierarchy.

In summary, each user sees a dedicated machine whose response times and charging rates are time varying. The service scheduling algorithm sees a set of unscheduled requests formed into a system of queues, where the queue discipline is a function of the decision rules, the priority rules, the attained service time, and an a priori estimate of service time. The resource scheduling algorithms see a system of queues of processors and storage spaces to be assigned to the flow of entering requests. The objective of the resource scheduling algorithms is to reduce service time. The objective of the service scheduling algorithm is to reduce the over-all cost of service; two indicators of the effectiveness are the sizes of the queues and the amount of time any request waits in queue. Choice of one algorithm generally affects performance achieved by the other.

3. GENERAL MATHEMATICAL MODEL

Models for time-shared computer systems may be broken into two classes: infinite input population and finite input population. Furthermore, the quantum service interval Q may be finite ($Q > 0$) or infinitesimal ($Q \to 0$);

this last we refer to as a processor-shared system. Based upon this breakdown, in Table 1 we summarize some of the many models that have been considered in the literature.* In all cases, except as noted, solutions are found for $T(t)$, which is the average response time (elapsed time between arrival of a request and its departure after complete service) given that its total service requirement is t seconds. Two other useful measures are T, the average response time (averaged over all service time requirements) and E, the expected number of requests waiting for or in service. The quantity g_{pn} in the table is defined below.

TABLE 1

Summary of Mathematical Queueing Models†

INFINITE POPULATION SOURCES

	$Q > 0$			$Q \to 0$	
Algo-rithm	g_{pn}	Reference and Comments	Algo-rithm	g_{pn}	Reference and Comments
RR	1	[2]	RR	1	[3]
RR	g_p	[3]	RR	g_p	[3]
FB$_N$	1	[4]	FB$_N$	1	[4]
			FCFS	1	[4]
FB$_\infty$	1	[4]	FB$_\infty$	1	[4]
FB$_\infty$	1	[4] Priority determines initial queue	FB$_\infty$	1	[4] Priority determines loading point
FB$_\infty$	g_{pn}	[5] Transform of response time obtained			
RR	Function of system state	[6]	RR	Function of system state	[6]
FB$_2$	Function of system state	[6]	FB$_2$	Function of system state	[6]
Wide class	g_{pn}	[7] Solves for attained service	Wide class	g_{pn}	[7] Solves for attained service
Wide class	g_{pn}	[8] States a conservation law	Wide class	g_{pn}	[8] States a conservation law

*This table is an expanded form of Table 1 in reference [1].

†RR is round-robin; FB$_N$ is multiple level (foreground-background) with N levels; and FCFS is first-come-first-served.

TABLE 1

SUMMARY OF MATHEMATICAL QUEUEING MODELS

INFINITE POPULATION SOURCES (cont.)

Q > 0			Q → 0		
Algo-rithm	g_{pn}	Reference and Comments	Algo-rithm	g_{pn}	Reference and Comments
FCFS	—	[9] Bribing model	FCFS	—	[9] Bribing model
RR	1	[10]	RR	1	[13] Solves for T
RR	1	[11] Includes swap-time	RR	1	[13] Solves for T
RR	1	[12] Includes swap-time	RR	1 also g_p for $P = 2$	[14] Obtains additional measures and comparisons
Wide class	g_{pn}	[7] Solves for attained service	Wide class	g_{pn}	[7] Solves for attained service

The usual approach taken in preparing a mathematical model for existing or proposed time-shared service facilities is to treat them as queueing systems. In these models a user request typically joins some queue, works its way up to the front of the queue, obtains service in the facility for some small amount of time (called a *quantum*), and then joins the same or some new queue to wait for more quanta if needed. The methods of queueing theory have been applied to a number of such models to obtain various measures of performance.

In order to generate and evaluate models of time-shared systems, we must gather data which describe the population of users. Such data then suggest idealizations we may use in our mathematical models and in our simulation models. They also allow us to compare assumed properties of the customers with the measurements.

We include in the class of queueing systems under consideration those with the following properties (see Fig. 1). We assume that the population of new arrivals to the system is separated into P priority groups, this priority being determined by some external property of the arrival (e.g., status in society, wealth, rank, size memory space required); the assumption here being that the required time in the service facility (e.g., total computation time) is known only to within a probability distribution. Accordingly, let (for $p = 1, 2, \ldots, P$)

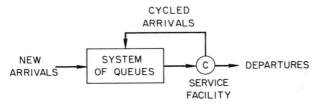

Fig. 1 Feedback queueing systems

$A_p(\theta) = P_r$ (customer from pth priority group requires think time $\leq \theta$)*

$1/\gamma_p$ = average think time for each customer from group p

λ_p = average arrival rate of customers to the system from the pth priority group (customers per second)

$B_p(t) = P_r$ (customer from pth priority group requires a total processing time $\leq t$)

$1/\mu_p$ = average service requirement (in operations, say additions, per customer) for customers from group p.

C = capacity of processor (in operations, say additions, per second).

Upon arrival to the system a new customer joins some queue in the system of queues. After some appropriate queueing discipline is followed, this customer will then be allowed into the service facility. On his first time through, if he is from priority group p, he will be allotted a maximum of $g_{p1}Q$ seconds of service where Q is a fixed time interval. If the quantum of time $g_{p1}Q$ is greater than or equal to his total required service time t he will then depart from the system as soon as he receives as much time as he needs; if $t > g_{p1}Q$, he will be cycled back to the system of queues where he joins some appropriate queue and waits for another quantum of service. On his nth visit to the service facility, this customer will receive a maximum of $g_{pn}Q$ seconds of service; thus if

$$Q \sum_{i=1}^{n-1} g_{pi} < t \leq Q \sum_{i=1}^{n} g_{pi}$$

this customer departs from the system during his nth quanta of service. If

$$t > Q \sum_{i=1}^{n} g_{pi}$$

he then recycles and continues.

*Think time is defined as the time it takes a customer to think up a new request for service after his last service request has been completed.

Whenever the service facility ejects a customer (either for departure or recycling), some customer (if one is available) is taken into service. The particular customer chosen depends upon the specific discipline used in arranging customers within the system of queues. No customers are allowed to leave before they receive their total required service (i.e., no defecting).

The source that generates the arrivals to the system has itself been modeled in two general ways. One assumption has been to consider that a finite number M of consoles is available and that the over-all arrival rate to the system is the sum of the individual arrival rates from each of the customers not presently in the system of queues or in the service facility. These systems are referred to as finite population models (see Fig. 2). A different assumption

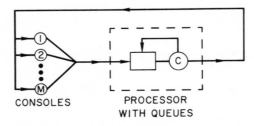

CONSOLES   PROCESSOR
WITH QUEUES

Fig. 2   Finite population model (the dashed box represents the system shown in Fig. 1).

can be made which considers an infinite population of users, in which case the average think time is taken to be infinite also, so that the average arrival rate of customers to the system is finite and fixed.

We note here that the limit that takes the finite population model into the infinite population model may be properly defined as follows: We consider the nonpriority ($P = 1$) case for simplicity. The total average arrival rate ($\lambda \equiv \sum \lambda_p$) for a finite number M of consoles is merely the average number of idle consoles E_I not in queue or in service times the average arrival rate γ, per idle console; i.e., $\lambda = \gamma E_I$. But, for T defined as the average response time

$$E_I = M \frac{1/\gamma}{T + (1/\gamma)}$$

since $1/\gamma$ is the average think time and $T + (1/\gamma)$ is the average cycle time back to a console. Thus, as $M \to \infty$ and $\gamma \to 0$, we have

$$\lambda = \lim_{\substack{M \to \infty \\ \gamma \to 0}} M\gamma \frac{1/\gamma}{T + (1/\gamma)} = \lim_{\substack{M \to \infty \\ \gamma \to 0}} M\gamma$$

since T, the average response time, is finite. This give us the average arrival rate for the infinite population systems.

In this same connection, we agree in all these models that the computing facility is not overloaded; i.e., if we define

$$\rho_p = \frac{\lambda_p}{\mu_p} C$$

and*

$$\rho = \sum_{p=1}^{p} \rho_p$$

then we insist that $\rho < 1$. This insures that the average work load (in operations per second) offered to the processor is less than its capacity to handle such a load.

In all of the following models the assumption is made that arrival time and processing time of a customer are independent random variables; also that these are independent of the values taken on by all other customers. Moreover, we recognize that whenever a customer is moved out of service and another is taken into service a period of time, called the *swap-time*, is required for the transfer. In many of the following models we assume for the sake of mathematical tractability that this cost, the swap-time, is zero. This assumption certainly should weaken the mathematical results. However, in the models involving a finite quantum Q we may think of a portion of that time as being used for swapping; this alters the service time distribution in a predictable way. In the processor-shared models ($Q \to 0$), the notion of swapping must be ignored; i.e., we insist that swap-time be zero. This is necessary since we are swapping at an infinite rate and since any nonzero swap-time would, by itself, overload the system. Thus in the zero swap-time models we obtain results that are idealized in the sense that any nonzero swap-time will only degrade the performance predicted; we recognize that our results are then upper bounds on performance.

In this general model we assume that the resource for which the users are competing is a *single* congestion point, say the central processing unit (CPU). Clearly, this is a gross simplification since there is also congestion at the input-output (I/O) interfaces as well as at all the various levels of memory in any real operating system. To date, this more complex system of queues

*Note that ρ_p equals average arrival rate of seconds of work to the computer from the pth group; so ρ is the total average arrival rate from all groups. Clearly, this must be less than unity for nonsaturation. Also, ρ_p is the fraction of time that the entire service facility is devoted to processing customers from the pth priority group; also ρ is the probability that the facility is nonempty.

within a computer has not been studied in depth, and so we confine ourselves to the simpler case of the CPU congestion.

We present below the results of analyses of a number of special cases of this general model.

4. SOME SPECIFIC MODELS AND RESULTS

INFINITE POPULATION MODELS

A number of papers have appeared in the literature on time-sharing describing models and results for the particular assumptions of infinite population sources. We consider some of these below:

1. The round-robin (RR) model [2]
   a. Discrete time model.
   Consider the original discrete time model of a time-shared processor first studied by Kleinrock [2] in 1964. In this model it is assumed that time is quantized with segments each Q seconds in length. At the end of each time interval, a new unit, or job, arrives in the system with probability λQ (result of a Bernoulli trial); thus, the average number of arrivals per second is λ. The service time (the required processing time) of a newly arriving unit is chosen independently from a geometric distribution such that for $0 \le \sigma < 1$

$$S_k = (1 - \sigma)\sigma^{k-1} \qquad k = 1, 2, 3, \ldots, \tag{1}$$

where S_k is the probability that a unit's service time is exactly k time intervals long (i.e., that its service time is kQ seconds). Thus we assume $P = 1$ (no priority distinction among the users) and $1/(\mu C) = Q\bar{k}$, where $\bar{k}$ is the average of k with respect to the S_k distribution, giving $1/(\mu C) = Q/(1 - \sigma)$. Also $A_p(\theta) = A(\theta)$ and $B_p(t) = B(t)$ are both discontinuous staircase functions given through the binomial and geometric distributions, respectively. Note also that $g_{pn} = 1$ for all p and n here. A unit whose processing requirement is kQ will be forced to join the first-come-first-served (FCFS) queue (see Fig. 3) k times in all before its service is completed.

For such a system it has been shown in [2] that the following holds:

THEOREM 1: The expected value, $T_{RR}(kQ)$, of the response time in the RR system for a job whose service time is kQ seconds, is

$$T_{RR}(kQ) = \frac{kQ}{1 - \rho} - \frac{\lambda Q^2}{1 - \rho}\left[1 + \frac{(1 - \sigma a)(1 - a^{k-1})}{(1 - \sigma)^2(1 - \rho)}\right] \tag{2}$$

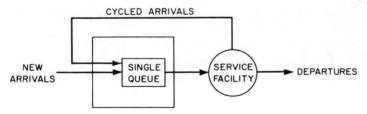

CYCLED ARRIVALS

Fig. 3   The RR system

where

$$a = \sigma + \lambda Q$$

and

$$\rho = \frac{\lambda Q}{1 - \sigma}$$

Furthermore, the expected number E_r of customers in the system is given by

$$E_r = \frac{\rho\sigma}{1 - \rho} \qquad (3)$$

THEOREM 2: The expected value $T'(kQ)$ of the response time in the strict FCFS system* for a unit whose service time is kQ seconds is

$$T'_{\text{FCFS}}(kQ) = \frac{QE_r}{1 - \sigma} + kQ \qquad (4)$$

where E_r is defined in Equation 3.

In reference [2] it is shown that a good approximation to $T_{\text{RR}}(kQ)$ is

$$T_{\text{RR}}(kQ) = kQE_r + kQ. \qquad (5)$$

When Equations 4 and 5 are compared, we see that for units which require a number of service intervals less (greater) than $1/(1 - \sigma)$, the RR waiting time is less (greater) than the strict FCFS system. One notes, however, that the average number of service intervals k is exactly $1/(1 - \sigma)$. Thus, for this

*This is a reference system and corresponds to the more usual case where a unit receives its complete processing requirement the first time it enters service. We assume that the input statistics here are identical to those for the RR system.

approximate solution, the crossover point for average waiting time is at the mean number of service intervals.

Curves of the RR system performance are given below in Fig. 4 where we plot $W(kQ) = T_{RR}(kQ) - kQ$, which is merely the average total time spent waiting *on the queue* for customers requiring kQ seconds of service.

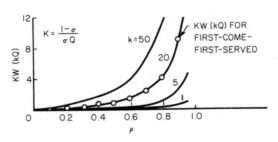

Fig. 4 $[(1 - \sigma)/\sigma Q]W(kQ)$ for late-arrival time-shared service system ($\sigma = 19/20$)

This figure shows the accuracy of our conclusion; namely, that the crossover point between RR and FCFS systems is at $k = \bar{k}$.

The quantum-controlled RR system has also been studied with both interarrival time distribution and service time distribution exponential (i.e., continuous rather than discrete as above). [4]

If we consider an RR system in which we allow $Q \to 0$, we arrive at an interesting model of a *processor*-shared system in which users are cycling around at an infinite rate, receiving an infinitesimal quantum of service infinitely often. When the total service time received equals a user's required processing time, he then leaves the system. Indeed, we see that this is identical to a model in which each user receives continuous processing at a rate C/n operations (say additions) per second when there are a total of n users in the system. The usefulness of this limit of processor sharing lies in its representation of an idealized sharing operation in which swap-time is assumed to be zero. For these cases, the natural analogue of the previous theorem is obtained.

b. Processor-shared model (no priorities).

If we assume zero swap-time, we may consider the case of an RR system in which $Q \to 0$. We must be careful in taking this limit, since the service time kQ also goes to zero in this case and our model loses all meaning. Consequently, let us agree to keep the average service time constant as $Q \to 0$. This involves changing σ, the decay rate in Equation 1 such that $\sigma \to 1$ as $Q \to 0$. Specifically, since we have $\bar{k} = 1/(1 - \sigma)$, let us define $1/\mu C =$

average service requirement (in seconds). We then obtain

$$\frac{1}{\mu C} = \frac{Q}{1-\sigma} = \text{constant as } Q \to 0 \text{ and } \sigma \to 1$$

or

$$\sigma = 1 - \mu C Q \tag{6}$$

Thus, the limiting operation we consider is where $Q \to 0$ and $\sigma \to 1$ in the manner expressed in Equation 6. The result of this limit is that the required service l (in operations) is exponentially distributed with parameter μ; namely,

$$p(l) = \mu e^{-\mu l} \tag{7}$$

where l is the length of the job.

We have chosen to assume that the length l of a job is given in number of operations instead of in seconds, thus making the user requirement independent of the machine on which it is serviced. Since C equals cpacity of a processor in operations (say, additions) per second, the service time for a job then becomes l/C seconds, with a mean service time of $1/(\mu C)$ seconds.

The arrival mechanism in the limit as $Q \to 0$ then becomes Poisson with an average arrival rate of λ customers per second. This model reduces to a system in which a user is processed at a rate C/n operations per second when there are n users sharing a computer of capacity C. This processing rate varies as new users enter and old ones leave the system. We are here assuming a harmonic variation of individual processing rate with number of customers (see Fig. 5).

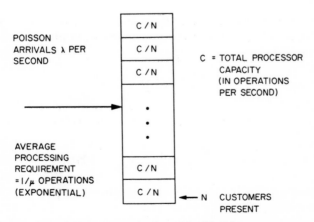

Fig. 5 Processor-shared model with N in system

For this system, we have the following theorem:

THEOREM 3: The expected value, $T(l/C)$, of the response time in the processor-shared system for a customer requiring l operations, is

$$T\frac{l}{C} = \frac{l/C}{1 - \rho} \tag{8}$$

where

$$\rho = \frac{\lambda}{\mu C}$$

The expected number E of customers in the system is

$$E = \frac{\rho}{1 - \rho} \tag{9}$$

c. The priority processor-shared system. [3]

In this system, there are P priority groups with Poisson arrivals at an average rate of λ_p per second and an exponentially distributed service requirement with a mean of $1/\mu_P$ operations $(p = 1, 2, \ldots, P)$. Assign a customer from the pth priority group a capacity f_pC when there are n_i customers in the system; f_p is given by

$$f_p = \frac{g_p}{\sum\limits_{i=1}^{P} g_i n_i} \tag{10}$$

For such a system,

THEOREM 4: The expected value $T_p(l/C)$ of the response time spent in the priority processor-shared system for a customer from priority group p who requires l operations is

$$T_p\frac{l}{C} = \frac{l}{C}\left[1 + \sum_{i=1}^{P} \frac{g_i \rho_i}{g_p(1 - \rho)}\right] \tag{11}$$

The expected number E_p of type p customers in the system is

$$E_p = \frac{\rho_p}{1 - \rho}\left[1 + \sum_{i=1}^{P}\left(\frac{g_i}{g_p} - 1\right)\rho_i\right] \tag{12}$$

See Fig. 6 on the following page for an example of $T_p(l/C)$.

d. FCFS model. [3]

For completeness, consider a strict FCFS system with the same input and service requirements as in our priority model.

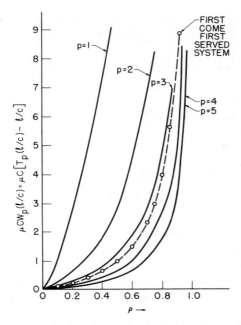

Fig. 6 Priority processor-shared system: performance as a function of p for $g_p = p^2$ $(p = 1, 2, 3, 4, 5)$, $\mu_p = \mu$, $\lambda_p = \lambda/P$, and $\mu l = 1$

THEOREM 5: The FCFS system with a priority input yields, for customers with l required operations, an expected response time as follows:

$$T\frac{l}{C} = \frac{l}{C} + \frac{\rho/\mu C}{1 - \rho} \tag{13}$$

where

$$\frac{1}{\mu C} = \frac{\rho}{\sum\limits_{p=1}^{P} \lambda_P}$$

Note that $P = 1$ yields the (nonpriority) processor-shared system.

5. THE MULTIPLE LEVEL PROCESSOR-SHARED MODEL [4, 5, 10]

This model, which is denoted by FB_N where N is the number of levels, is shown in Fig. 7. Assume exponential interarrival and service times. A unit at the service point at any given queue level will not be serviced unless all

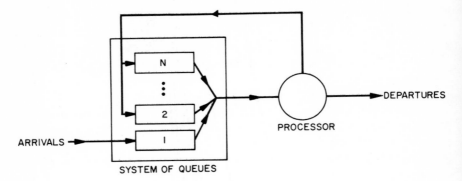

Fig. 7 The FB_N model

lower numbered queues are empty. Thus, immediately after a unit has received service, the next unit serviced will be the one at the service point of the lowest level, nonempty queue. This unit will be given a quantum Q of service as in the RR model; if more is needed, then the unit is subsequently placed at the end of the next higher level queue; otherwise it leaves the system.

For $N < \infty$ assume that the Nth level queue is a quantum-controlled, FCFS queue. Specifically, units at the Nth level are served a quantum at a time until completion (i.e., there is no RR in the Nth queue but an arrival to a lower level during the servicing of an Nth level unit will preempt this unit after it has completed the quantum service in progress). Note that, with these assumptions, FB_1 denotes the conventional FCFS system.

The average response time $T(t)$ has been obtained for $Q > 0$ (see [4]). Below are given results only for the processor-sharing limit $Q \to 0$. For finite N the FB_N system reduces to a FCFS system. Of greater interest is the limiting case $Q = 0$ when we assume $N = \infty$. By arguments based on very small Q sizes it can be seen that the resulting system can be viewed as corresponding to a system in which arrivals always preempt the unit, if any, in service and are allowed service until their service time exceeds that having been received by some other unit in the queue. We have the following theorem from [4].

THEOREM 6: The average response time for customers requiring t seconds of service in the processor-shared FB_N system is

$$T(t) = \begin{cases} \dfrac{1}{1-\rho}\dfrac{1}{\mu} & N < \infty \\[2ex] \dfrac{\dfrac{\lambda}{2}\displaystyle\int_0^t x^2\,dF(x)}{[1-\rho(1-\epsilon^{-\mu t})]^2} + \dfrac{t}{1-\rho(1-\epsilon^{-\mu t})} & N = \infty \end{cases} \tag{14}$$

where

$$F(x) = \begin{cases} 0 & X < 0 \\ 1 - \epsilon^{-\mu x} & 0 \leq x < t \\ 1 & x < t \end{cases} \tag{15}$$

Coffman [15] has also considered such systems with externally assigned priorities. These priorities determine the initial queue a customer joins upon entry to the FB_N system (the lower priority units join higher numbered, lower priority queues). He also carries this extension to the processor-shared case.

Schrage [5] has also considered such systems in greater generality. He has generalized the quanta to depend upon n; i.e., $g_{pn} = g_n$. Also he allows an arbitrary service distribution $B(t)$. However, he restricts his investigation only to the infinite level case $N = \infty$. Schrage solves for the Laplace transform of the response time and this allows him to obtain the moments of this measure. In particular, he obtains the mean and variance.

Figure 8 shows a comparison between the RR and FB_∞ case for $Q \to 0$; these two are also compared to the shortest-job-first (SJF) system in which

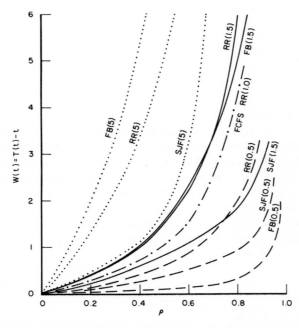

Fig. 8 Comparison of waiting times for various scheduling algorithms

prior knowledge of a job's service time is assumed known. The notation is such that RR(5) labels the curve for RR requiring 5 seconds of service time.

FINITE POPULATION MODELS

One of the first principal models in this category has been studied by Scherr. [13] He assumes that think time and service are both independently and exponentially distributed. A total of M consoles (see Fig. 2) is assumed to be available and a nonpriority processor-shared system is considered; i.e., $Q \to 0, g_{pn} = 1$. His main result, for a single processor, is given in the following theorem.

THEOREM 7:

$$T = \frac{M/\mu C}{1 - \pi_0} - \frac{1}{\gamma} \tag{16}$$

where

$$\pi_0 = Pr \text{ (no customers are receiving or awaiting service)}$$

$$= \left[\sum_{j=0}^{M} \frac{M!}{(M - j)} \left(\frac{\gamma}{\mu C} \right)^j \right]^{-1} \tag{17}$$

and

$$\frac{1}{\gamma} = \text{average think time}$$

Here we give a simple and instructive proof of this theorem. Since the system is assumed to be in the steady state, we may use the fact that the rate at which customers enter the system (the dashed box in Fig. 2) equals the rate at which they depart from the system. The fraction of time that a console is not in the system (i.e., it is in the thinking state) is merely the ratio of the average time $1/\gamma$ that it spends thinking to the average time $T + (1/\gamma)$ it spends in making a complete round trip. Each of M consoles generates requests (leaves the thinking state) at a rate γ per second, providing such a customer is in the thinking state (the probability that it is thinking is the fraction described above). Thus, the input rate of customers to the system is

$$M\gamma \frac{1/\gamma}{(1/\gamma) + T}$$

When m customers are in the system (probability m) then the rate at which each customer is being ejected is* $(\mu C)/m$. Since there are m such, the average output rate of customers is

$$\sum_{m=1}^{M} \frac{\mu C}{m} m \pi_m = \mu C(1 - \pi_0)$$

Equating the input and output rates, we find that

$$T = \frac{M}{\mu C(1 - \pi_0)} - \frac{1}{\gamma} \tag{18}$$

The expression given for π_0 is trivially obtained from any text on queueing theory (such as p. 121 of [17]).

We note here that as $M \to \infty$, $\gamma \to 0$, such that $M\gamma = \lambda$, we arrive at the infinite population model of a nonpriority processor-shared system as follows: From Equation (17) we have

$$\pi_0^{-1} = \sum_{j=0}^{M} \frac{M(M-1)\cdots(M-j+1)}{M(M)\cdots(M)} \left(\frac{M\gamma}{\mu C}\right)^j$$

$$= \sum_{j=0}^{M} \left(1 - \frac{1}{M}\right)\left(1 - \frac{2}{M}\right)\cdots\left(1 - \frac{j-1}{M}\right)\rho^j$$

where we define $\rho = M\gamma/\mu C$. Continuing,

$$\pi_0^{-1}$$

$$= \frac{(1-\rho) + \sum_{j=1}^{M}\left[\left(1 - \frac{1}{M}\right)\cdots\left(1 - \frac{j-1}{M}\right)\rho^j - \left(1 - \frac{1}{M}\right)\cdots\left(1 - \frac{j-1}{M}\right)\rho^{j+1}\right]}{(1-\rho)}$$

$$= \frac{1 - \rho + \rho + \sum_{j=1}^{M} \rho^{j+1}\left(1 - \frac{1}{M}\right)\cdots\left(1 - \frac{j-1}{M}\right)\left(1 - \frac{j}{M} - 1\right)}{1 - \rho}$$

thus

$$\lim_{\substack{M \to \infty \\ \gamma \to 0}} \pi_0 = \lim_{\substack{M \to \infty \\ \gamma \to 0}} \frac{1 - \rho}{1 - \sum_{j=1}^{M} \rho^{j+1}\left(1 - \frac{1}{M}\right)\cdots\left(1 - \frac{j-1}{M}\right)\frac{j}{M}}$$

$$= \lim_{\substack{M \to \infty \\ \gamma \to 0}} \frac{1 - \rho}{1 - \frac{1}{M}\sum_{j=1}^{M} j\rho^{j+1}}$$

*The quantity $1/(\mu C)$ is the ratio of average number of operations per customer $(1/\mu)$ to the number of operations per second (C), giving the average number of seconds of service per customer (when he is provided with a capacity of size C). The inverse, μC, is the rate at which he is completed. When provided with a capacity of C/m, his output rate is $(\mu C)/m$.

thus

$$\lim_{\substack{M\to\infty \\ \gamma\to 0}} \pi_0 = \frac{1-\rho}{1-\frac{1}{M}\left(\frac{\rho}{1-\rho}\right)^2} \tag{19}$$

Applying this last to Equation 18 gives, for $M \to \infty$, $\gamma \to 0$,

$$T = \frac{1/(\mu C)}{1-\rho} \tag{20}$$

Inspection of Equation 8 reveals that the average response time for all jobs (averaged over service requirements) yields exactly T as above in Equation 20. Furthermore, in the limit, it is easy to show that

$$E = \frac{\rho}{1-\rho}$$

as in Equation 9. This confirms the agreement between the two models in the limit.

Scherr also derives a similar expression for T in the case where the processing facility consists of more than one processor.

Greenberger [10] has considered a finite population model with an RR scheduling algorithm under exponential assumptions of think time and serivce time with a finite quantum Q. In addition, he includes a swap-time of V seconds. He obtains an approximation that can be used to obtain the response time conditioned on the serivce time kQ as

$$T(kQ) = \frac{k}{\mu C}(1 - e^{-\mu CQ} + \mu CV)\left[\frac{M}{1-\pi_0} - \frac{(\mu C)'}{\gamma}\right]$$

$$+ \left(\frac{1-\pi'_0\left(1+\frac{M\gamma}{(\mu C)'}\right)}{1-\pi'_0}\right)\left(\frac{S_2 + V^2}{2(S_1 + V)} - S_1\right) \tag{21}$$

where

$$\frac{1}{(\mu C)'} = \frac{1}{\mu C} + \frac{V}{1 - e^{-\mu CQ}}$$

$$S_1 = \frac{1}{\mu C} + (1 - e^{-\mu CQ})$$

$$S_2 = \frac{2}{\mu C}(S_1 - Qe^{-\mu CQ})$$

and where π'_0 is the expression for π_0 given in Equation 17 with μC replaced by $(\mu C)'$. A similar model has also been studied by Patel [16]. In Equation 21 as $V \to 0$, $Q \to 0$, we note that $T(kQ)$ averaged over k reduces to the expression in Equation 16 given by Scherr for the processor-shared systems. The same comment applies when one takes this to the limit of an infinite population system, obtaining Equation 20 above.

In 1966 an excellent paper was published by Krishnamoorthi and Wood [11] in which they first considered the model Greenberger later studied. They obtained results for two measures of cycle time as well as various moments of the queue size. They also include a fixed swap-time.

More recently Adiri and Avi-Itzhak [12] studied the same model and obtained additional results in similar directions.

Let us now return to the expression for T given in Equation 18. This result was first used by Scherr [13] for time-shared systems. Scherr also tested the worth of this model in the MIT time-sharing system described in greater detail below. His principal finding is shown in Fig. 9 where he has compared the results of measurement (shown as dotted data points and the least-squares fit B-B to these points) with the results of model analysis given by Equation

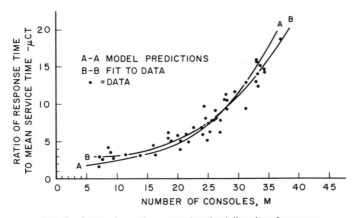

Fig. 9 Comparison of measured and predicted performance

18 above (curve A-A). As can be seen, the normalized* response time μCT is accurately predicted by our model, in spite of the fact that the MIT time-sharing system does not operate according to the assumptions of the model.

Due to the finite value of M, one questions whether it is possible to *saturate* the system. Indeed, if we define saturation as that point where the system goes unstable in some sense, such as average response time growing to

*If provided the full capacity, a customer will spend an average of $1/(\mu C)$ seconds in the system. We choose to normalize T with respect to this giving μCT which represents the factor by which a customer is delayed (because of sharing the system) in relation to his time in system without sharing.

infinity, then we see immediately that our system is never saturated, for $\gamma/(\mu C) < \infty$. (We have seen that such unstable behavior is possible in the infinite population case.) Nevertheless there does exist an appropriate definition of saturation as follows (see Kleinrock [14]): If we replace each service time by its average $1/(\mu C)$, and if we schedule the arrivals to occur uniformly in time, each spending exactly $1/\gamma$ seconds thinking, then we see that the system can handle at most a number of consoles M^* given by

$$M^* = \frac{1/(\mu C) + 1/\gamma}{1/(\mu C)} = \frac{\mu C + \gamma}{\gamma} \tag{22}$$

without any mutual interference. This definition is similar to that given by Scherr. [13] For example, if each customer requires 35 seconds for thinking and 1 second for computation, then 36 such customers can be handled. This provides the basis on which we define M^* as the saturation point for our M-console system. We plot Equation 18 again in Fig. 10 where $M^* = 41$ [$1/(\mu C) = 0.88$, $1/\gamma = 35.2$]. We see that μCT begins to increase sharply in the vicinity $M \approx M^*$. For $M \ll M^*$ μCT grows very slowly, since customers tend to request computation during other customers' think-time.

For $M \gg M^*$, we see from Equations 17 and 18 that

$$\mu CT \cong M - M^* + 1 \tag{23}$$

since $\pi_0 \to 0$. This asymptote is shown dashed in Fig. 10, and we observe that it intersects the line $\mu CT = 1$ at $M = M^*$, since

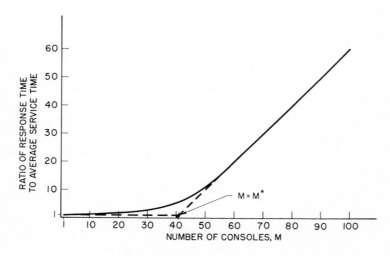

Fig. 10   Performance and saturation

$$M^* - \frac{\mu C}{\gamma} = 1$$

Since the slope of this asymptote is 1, it shows that each additional user completely interferes with all the other users, adding one more unit of normalized delay to μCT. The fact that the asymptote crosses $\mu CT = 1$ at precisely M^* shows, for $M \gg M^*$, that the system has absorbed M^* users and converted them into one user and is now experiencing complete interference among the other $M - M^*$ users (i.e., the additional delay added to the response time for each user is $M - M^*$, since, from Equation 23, $\mu CT \cong 1 + M - M^*$).

It is interesting to observe the degradation in performance when we split the system of M consoles and a processor of capacity C (referred to as an (M, C) system) into two $(M/2, C/2)$ systems (see Fig. 11). More generally, we consider $N(M/N, C/N)$ systems (N a positive integer).

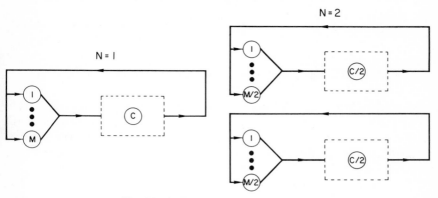

Fig. 11   Comparative systems ($N = 1, 2$)

Let T_N be the behavior (average delay) of an $(M/N, C/N)$ system. Let us consider this degradation, as N increases, by plotting $\Delta_N = (T_N - T_1)/T_1$ versus M. This is the normalized increase in response time due to splitting the system. Figure 12 shows this for $N = 2, 3, 4, 5$, and 10. We see that the degradation is large for $M \ll M^*$. Note for $M \gg M^*$ that $\Delta_N \to 0$; this says in the heavily saturated case that the (M, C) and $(M/N, C/N)$ systems both behave the same from the user's viewpoint. The inflection point in Δ_N is seen to occur in the vicinity $M \approx M^*$, indicating that the comparative degradation is most sensitive to a change in M in this vicinity.

ADDITIONAL RESULTS

The distribution of attained service has been defined as (see [7]) $N_p(\tau) =$ expectation of the number of customers in the system of queues and in service

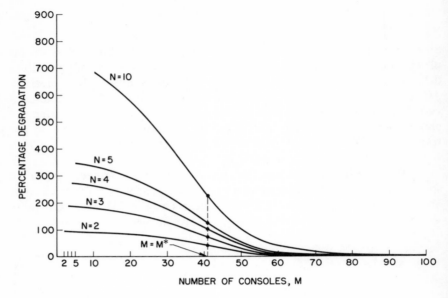

Fig. 12 Percentage degradation of comparative systems (N = 2, 3, 4, 5, 10)

from priority group p who have so far received exactly τ seconds of service.

This quantity, $N_p(\tau)$, gives one a description of the composition of the various queues and a measure of the relative state of partial service received by those customers still in the system. The results for attained service are very general.

There also exists [8] a conservation law which states that an appropriate average of the mean response times (by priority) can be invariant to scheduling algorithm.

Coffman [6] has considered models for $Q > 0$ and $Q \to 0$ with variable quanta for both RR and FB$_2$ in which a customer in service receives an additional quantum for each new customer who enters while he is in service. This tends to reduce the swap-time.

The notion of paying a price for one's priority is not an unfamiliar one—it is often referred to as bribing. [9] A bribing model has been considered in which customers offer a bribe (based upon an impatience factor of their own) to gain preferred position on line. All those bribing strategies are then characterized which minimize an appropriately defined cost function averaged over the population of users.

When we consider more than a single processor, a number of possibilities present themselves. We may choose to use all processors in parallel, with or without constraints (see Coffman [15]) or in series (see Kleinrock [18]) or in some series-parallel combination (see [19, 20]). The problem associated with providing the interconnection of a network of processors is a major one; some work along these lines may be found in [20, 21].

6. MEASUREMENTS AND SIMULATION

Measurements made on actual time-shared systems or on simulated models of time-shared systems have the following purposes:

1. To make a choice between one system and another.
2. To deepen the understanding of a system so as to affect the design of other systems or to optimize a given system.

In the first case the user is interested in measurements of response time and both the cost and quality of the system. In the second case the model builder is interested in measurements of those parameters that arise in his model and that can be subjected to reasonable measurement. Examples of the latter measurements are the average number of active consoles, queue size, waiting time in queue, response time, service time, and think time. In this case the system designer is interested in measurements that are easy to make that most directly lead to optimization techniques as well as support the building of models. These last measurements will therefore be concerned with the efficiency of processor and storage allocation in addition to the scheduling algorithm affecting the input queue.

Here we seek to integrate a number of simulation and measurement results, which have appeared in the literature. Table 2 summarizes reported measurements of user characteristics, and Table 3 summarizes reported measurements of performance characteristics. In both cases references are denoted with italic type indicating simulation and roman type indicating actual system measurements.*

TABLE 2

DATA ON USER CHARACTERISTICS

User Characteristic	Reference
Probability Distribution of Think Time	S, T
Probability Distribution of Service Time	C, S, T
Probability Distribution of Program Size	C, S, T
Priority vs. Program Size	SD
Percentage User Time vs. Day	SD
Probability Distribution of Disc Requests	C

*These results are taken from [1] as was Table 1.

TABLE 3

DATA ON PERFORMANCE CHARACTERISTICS

Performance Characteristic	*Reference*
Response Time/Processor Time vs. M	S, T, *S*
Response Time vs. Processor Time	*S*
Response Time vs. M	*T*, R
Probability Distribution of Response Time	*S*, L
$\bar{M}$ vs. M	S, *S*
Probability Distribution of M	T, *TR*
$\bar{M}$ vs. Q	*TM*
Computer Utilization vs. M	S, *S*, *TR*
Computer Utilization vs. Q	*TM*
Breakdown of Computer Utilization vs. Processor Time	C
Batch Processing RR Computer Utilization Change	T, *TM*
Tape Usage vs. M	T
Utilization of Swap Storage vs. M	S
User, Idle, and Disk Time vs. Day	SD
Breakdown of Computer Time Usage	S
Memory Map vs. Program Size	SD

First, the essential characteristics of a number of experiments and then the measurement results are discussed below.

THE EXPERIMENTS

We consider the results of four simulation efforts and four measurement efforts. Among the simulations, we have:

1. Scherr (S) [13] has simulated the MIT Project MAC's Compatible Time-Shared System (CTSS—see Corbato [22]). The CTSS scheduling algorithm is a variation on the FB_9 system described earlier with $g_{pn} = 2^{n-1}$ and $Q = 0.5$ seconds; the variation includes a priority system in which program length is used to place new programs onto the various queues (longer length receiving lower priority). He considers these simulation models: CTSS; CTSS with RR ($g_{pn} = 1$, $Q = 2$ seconds) instead of FB_9; and CTSS with multiprogramming to provide overlapped processing and swapping.

2. Fine and McIsaac (F.M.) have simulated a system similar to the SDC Time-Sharing System. [23] They consider an RR system as well as a two-queue scheduling procedure (similar to FB_2). The second (lower priority) queue contains customers who have submitted production jobs and who are

serviced to completion (FCFS) during the idle intervals between "nonproduction" jobs which are served RR on the first queue (high priority).

3. Fife and Rosenberg (F.R.) [24] have simulated a system in which the central notion is one of memory sharing with fixed memory partitioning. The main core is divided into five memory blocks. Each user is confined to remain within a single block. Jobs queue up for an allocation to core memory, and, once in core, remain there until the job is completed or until the program halts awaiting an operator message (or until an illegal command is generated). Processing is transferred to a new job in core when the current program being run fills its output buffer.

4. Lavita (L) [25] has simulated an FCFS run-to-completion system with emphasis on the comparison between a drum system and a disk system.

Among the actual system measurement efforts, we include the following:

1. Scherr (S) [13] has made measurements of the behavior and system performance on the MIT Project MAC's CTSS [22] as described earlier. During the period of his measurements CTSS served approximately 250 users with an IBM 7094 (augmented with disk and drum storage) connected through an IBM 7750 transmission controller to users' remote consoles (each consisting of a keyboard and printer). The core memory consisted of 2 modules, each of 32,768 36-bit words, with an access time of 2 microseconds (the first module held only the supervisory program and the other was used for users' programs during excution).

2. Totschek (T) [26] reports measurements made on the SDC Time-Sharing System [27] which can handle up to 35 users at teletypes at remote consoles. Inputs from the user consoles pass through a D.E.C. PDP-1 computer to the central processor. The central processor is an IBM manufactured AN/FSQ-32, which contains 65,536 48-bit words of high speed memory (of which 48,784 are available for user programs) with a cycle time of 2.5 microseconds. A high speed buffer of 16,384 words is the interface between the AN/FSQ-32 and the PDP-1. Two scheduling algorithms are used. The first is an RR scheme (with $g_{pn} = 1$, Q = 400 milliseconds). The second is an FB_2 system where $g_{p1} = 1$, $g_{p2} = 50$; the second queue is automatically interrupted (pre-empted) when the first queue becomes nonempty.

3. Sutherland (SD) [28] has made measurements on the Lawrence Radiation Laboratory (LRL) Time-Shared System which is implemented on the CDC 6600. The system handles 48 teletype-equipped consoles which serve 110 users. Each console connects to one of 10 peripheral processors (each containing 4096 12-bit words). One other of these peripheral processors carries out the scheduling task. The mass memory is a disk. Central memory consists of 30,000 words reserved for supervisory tables and 100,000 words available to

the user. Up to 10 users may be in this second section of memory at any one time. The scheduling algorithm among these 10 is RR priority system with $g_{pn} = p$, $Q = 40$ milliseconds. Loading of new programs is done on a priority as well as an available memory space basis. Every 3.75 seconds the system does a priority load which removes a lower priority job if, by so doing, a higher priority job can be loaded and run. This is subject to the guarantee that a program will not be dumped for a number of microseconds equal to $128p$ times the program size (in code words). Each user is charged (against his daily allotment) an amount of time equal to his central processor time (CPU) plus his input-output time (I/O) times his priority p; i.e., (CPU + I/O)p minutes. A user's priority is self-assigned!

4. Cantrell (C) [29] has reported on his measurements of the GE-Dartmouth Time-Shared System. This system handles 200 users at remote teletype terminals. Inputs from user terminals are processed by GE D-30's en route to the central processor. Two D-30's are at Dartmouth for their users. One D-30 is at Boston and one D-30 is at New York City for GE users. The central processor consists of one GE 635 with 65,536 36-bit words of high speed memory (of which 25K are available for user programs) with a cycle time of 2 microseconds. The memory hierarchy consists of two Disks (16M each), Drum (50,000 words), six Tape Drives and an RCA RACE file (340M characters). The system uses a simple RR scheduling algorithm. Each user gets a fixed 200 millisecond quantum.

RESULTS OF SIMULATION AND MEASUREMENT

The data obtained falls into two categories—user characteristics and performance characteristics; we list these obtained data in Table 2 and Table 3 respectively. We define $\bar{M}$ as the number of active consoles* and M as the average value of $\bar{M}$. The characteristics listed in these tables refer to graphs, figures, or tables in the references cited.

Of primary interest with respect to user characteristics is the distribution of interarrival times (or think times). One finds a fair degree of agreement between the two sources of measurement, and it is interesting to note that both yield an average think time of approximately 35 seconds.† In these two cases the standard deviation of think time was the same order of magnitude as the average. Both sources show curves that seem to indicate that the think times are approximately exponentially distributed.

The other major user characteristic is the distribution of service time (swap time excluded). The three sets of data agree to some extent here, all ranging over several orders of magnitude with slowly decreasing tails. The

---

*This reflects the load on the system.

†In fact, Scherr found this mean value to vary only slightly with time of day, day of week, and number of active consoles.

median falls around 0.05 seconds, with much larger variances. The mean values do not agree to well, but this variation is understandable due to the great sensitivity of the mean to the details at the tail of the distribution. Totschek comments that the log-normal distribution fits both service time and think time reasonably well. It seems that a hyperexponential distribution would do well also. Cantrell observes that the shortest 90 per cent of all service times represents just slightly more than 10 per cent of the system load (in processor time) and, therefore, that the longest 10 per cent account for almost 90 per cent of the load (compute time)!

The distribution of program sizes provides little agreement among the sources. Scherr reports an average program size of 6.3×10^3 words.

A thorough discussion of the wealth of information available on performance characteristics listed in Table 3 can provide a basis for many future papers. Rich as these data are, a great deal remains to be done, not only in making additional measurements, but also in determining more compact measures of time-shared system performance. We choose to discuss only certain highlights of the data in Table 3.

One of the most significant observations one can make is with respect to the first item in Table 3. The results given by Scherr for the ratio of response time to processor time as a function of M for the CTSS measured data, the CTSS simulation, and the RR simulation all agree remarkably well. Furthermore, they all agree with his RR processor-shared model! Totschek's curves are similar in shape to Scherr's, but an absolute comparison is difficult to make because Totschek includes I/O time in the response time.

A quantity that is difficult to solve for analytically from the mathematical models is the probability density function of the response time (usually only its mean value T is found). This density can be obtained through simulation however, and both Scherr and Lavita have done this. In the CTSS and RR cases Scherr obtains a function which looks like an exponential distribution. For a FCFS algorithm Lavita obtains a distinctly different distribution, which shows very few short response times; this is easily seen to be due to the relatively long waits that even short jobs must experience due to the run-to-completion rule.

The remaining measurements concerned with system performance are widely dispersed in character and of a probing nature rather than strongly relevant to some model. They reflect the observations of Estrin, et al. [30] that present methods of measurement do not allow sufficient freedom in design of experiments on complex systems.

Now let us consider the relevancy of the tabulated measurements to the previously discussed models and vice versa. The infinite population model cannot be used to predict the characteristics of a finite console system of the types measured. These systems inherently reduce the arrival rate of requests as the number of busy consoles approaches the total number of consoles;

i.e., they are self-correcting. However, in the case of a large information processing utility we may well see a system with a huge number of terminals most of which are idle at any one time. In such a case the infinite population model assumptions would hold. This would be the case $M \to \infty$, $\gamma \to 0$ discussed in the third section. Therefore it is apparent form Table 1 that much of the work on modeling has been dealing only with a futuristic condition.

In the case of the finite population models it can be ovserved that:

1. Scherr has demonstrated predictability of his model. It might be of interest to explore the effectiveness of Scherr's adjustment for swap-time under conditions of varying Q.

2. In the case of Greenberger's model, which includes the effect of swap-time under assumptions of round robin and exponential service time and think time, some computation could explore the predictability.

3. In the multiprocessor case both models and simulated or constructed systems are too sparse at the present time to expect many results.

7. CONCLUSIONS

All presently proposed time-shared computer systems consider scheduling algorithms which favor the short problems. It seems apparent that any information processing utility to be established must deal with an environment which attracts all large customer groups.

Unfortunately, almost any current or proposed scheduling algorithm can be "defeated" to some degree by an intelligent "countermeasure" on the part of a clever user (see Coffman and Kleinrock [31]).

Most of the weakness in the relevancy of measurements to models arises, at present, from the unavailability of tools for making desired observations of dynamic systems. The recent concentration of some studies [30] on the use of a computer to observe others as well as the identification of methods for useful self-measurement gives some hope of progress in this area.

A particularly significant ingredient is still lacking in this field. It is the careful description of an *appropriate cost function* for time-shared systems. Greenberger [10] discusses this somewhat. So far, we have been able to do a reasonable job of *analyzing* a variety of scheduling algorithms for time-shared processors. However, we cannot *synthesize* such systems in an optimum fashion until a suitable criteria (cost function) is chosen.

REFERENCES

1. ESTRIN, G., and L. KLEINROCK, "Measures, Models and Measurements for Time-Shared Computer Utilities," *Proceedings of the 22nd National Conference of the Association for Computing Machinery* (August 1967), pp. 85-96.

2. KLEINROCK, L., "Analysis of a Time-Shared Processor," *Naval Research Logistic Quarterly,* XI (1964), 59-73.

3. KLEINROCK, L., "Time-Shared Systems; A Theoretical Treatment," *JACM,* XIV, No. 2 (April 1967), 242-61

4. COFFMAN, E. G., and L. KLEINROCK, "Some Feedback Queueing Models for Time-Shared Systems," *JACM* (forthcoming).

5. SCHRAGE, L. E., "The Queue M/G/1 with Feedback to Lower Priority Queues," *Management Science,* XII, Series A (1967), 466-74.

6. COFFMAN, E. G., "Analysis of Two Time-Sharing Algorithms Designed for Limited Swapping,"*JACM* (forthcoming).

7. KLEINROCK, L., "Distribution of Attained Service in Time-Shared Systems," *J. of Computers and Systems Science,* I, No. 3 (October 1967), 287-98.

8. KLEINROCK, L., "A Conservation Law for a Wide Class of Queueing Disciplines," *Naval Research Logistics Quarterly,* XII, No. 2 (June 1965), 181-92.

9. KLEINROCK, L., "Optimum Bribing for Queue Position," *J. of the Operations Research Society of America,* XV, No. 2 (March-April 1967), 304-18.

10. GREENBERGER, M., "The Priority Problem and Computer Time-Sharing," *Management Science,* XII (1966), 888-906.

11. KRISHNAMOORTHI, B., and R. G. WOOD, "Time-Shared Operations with Both Interarrival and Service Time Exponential," *JACM,* XIII, No. 3 (July 1966), 317-38

12. ADIRI, I., and B. AVI-ITZHAK, "A Time-Sharing Queue with a Finite Number of Customers," *Report from the Technion* (Israel Institute of Technology), Operations Research, Statistics and Economics Mimeograph Series No. 10.

13. SCHERR, A. L., "An Analysis of Time-Shared Computer Systems," *MIT Research Monograph No. 36.*

14. KLEINROCK, L., "Certain Analytic Results for Time-Shared Processors," *Proceedings of the IFIPS '68 Congress* (August 5-10), 1968.

15. COFFMAN, E. G., "Stochastic Models of Multiple and Time-Shared Computer Operations," *UCLA Department of Engineering Report No. 66-38* (June 1966).

16. PATEL, N. R., "A Mathematical Analysis of Computer Time-Shared Systems," Master's thesis, Massachusetts Institute of Technology, 1964.

17. SAATY, T. L., *Elements of Queueing Theory.* New York: McGraw-Hill Book Company, 1961.

18. KLEINROCK, L., "Sequential Processing Machines (S.P.M.) Analyzed with a Queueing Theory Model," *JACM,* XIII, No. 2 (April 1966), 179-93.

19. BUSSELL, B., "Properties of a Variable Structure Computer System in the Solution of Parabolic Partial Differential Equations." Ph.D. dissertation, University of California, Los Angeles, 1962.

20. FORD, L. R., JR., and D. R. FULKERSON, *Flows in Networks*. New Jersey: Princeton University Press, 1962.

21. KLEINROCK, L., *Communication Nets; Stochastic Message Flow and Delay*. New York: McGraw-Hill Book Company, 1964.

22. CORBATO, F. J., ET AL., *The Compatible Time-Sharing System*. M.I.T. Press, Cambridge, 1962.

23. FINE, G. H., and P. V. McISSAC, "Simulation of a Time-Sharing System," *SDC Report SP-1909* (December 1964).

24. FIFE, D., and R. ROSENBERG, "On Queueing in a Memory Shared Computer." *Proceedings of 19th National Congress of the ACM* (August 1964), pp. H1-1 to H1-12.

25. LAVITA, P. P., "Digital Simulation of a Time-Shared System." Master's thesis, New York University, 1966.

26. TOTSCHEK, R. A., "An Empirical Investigation into the Behavior of the SDC Time-Sharing System," *SDC Report* SP-2191 (August 1965).

27. COFFMAN, E. G., J. I. SCHWARTZ, and C. WEISSMAN, "A General-Purpose Time-Sharing System," *Proceedings of the Spring Joint Computer Conference*, XXV (1964), 397-411.

28. SUTHERLAND, G. G., talk presented at the Workshop on Models for Time-Shared Processing in the Symposium on Computers and Communications; Their System Interaction, IEEE Communications Technology Group and the Computer Group, January 1967.

29. CANTRELL, H., talk presented at Workshop on Models for Time-Shared Processing in Symposium in Ref. 28.

30. ESTRIN, G., D. HOPKINS, B. COGGAN, and S. CROCKER, "Snuper Computer— A Computer Instrumentation Automaton," *AFIPS Conference Proceedings*, XXX (1967), 645-56.

31. COFFMAN, E. G., and L. KLEINROCK, "Computer Scheduling Methods and their Countermeasures," *Proceedings of the Spring Joint Computer Conference*, XXXII (1968), 11-21.

Data Base Management:

The Keystone of Applied System Architecture

CHARLES W. BACHMAN

General Electric Company
Phoenix, Arizona

There are two strong trends in the information processing industry today. One of these is the move from the traditional batch sequential processing mode toward on-line direct access. The second is toward using information processing equipment to help business management to control and plan operations in their business. I believe that both of these trends, the one toward on-line batch processing and the one toward the "main line" application, must be followed. Main line here is used in the same sense as the Pennsylvania Railroad runs through Philadelphia to the West. That's where the bulk of the traffic goes, the main line. I think the bulk of our traffic in business is in the area of operational control, be it command and control in a military sense or order processing and manufacturing control in a manufacturing industry. I believe that these trends are not only true but also that they must be evolutionary. During the transition period we will be going through, the computer users will be desperately looking for direction, direction on how they should be designing and implementing these information systems, how they should use all the new hardware devices and all the new software systems effectively. The user, and industry as a whole, needs a powerful new concept of how all these tools, the hardware, system software, and the application fit together into a total system structure that meets the user's needs and wants.

Let us start with that user and take a look at what makes him tick. Most of these users are businessmen, businessmen who are struggling to survive in what seems to be a hostile environment. They are caught in a squeeze play of lower prices and rising costs. They are being pressured for greater variety of products and services for their customers. They must cope with fluctuating demands, higher taxes, labor problems, and a great variety of factors all of which put the typical businessman into a very difficult situation. They are looking for help.

About ten years ago, a new problem solving tool arrived on the scene—the computer. It has been a great help in solving large, complex computing problems. It has also been some help, not much, to the business-oriented user. Although he has applied it primarily to the routine data processing needs, not to the main line of business, it has reduced clerical cost, but in general it has not significantly affected the performance, the profit, or the gross sales of his business. In order to make it easier for the user to utilize this hardware, he is now being provided with system software—compilers, operating systems, data management systems, communications software, etc. that allow him to do multiprogramming, multiprocessing, and therefore, help him to solve his business problems. These new aids have been of some help to the users and have, in general, helped him to reduce somewhat his implementation costs. They are also however, introducing a greater degree of complexity into his planning and implementation of information systems. Hardware and system software do not alone get the user's job done. Only when the application has been designed and fitted to the system software and hardware does a customer have something of value in his business. We call the total combination of hardware, systems software, and application an *applied* system as opposed to merely a computer system. Our premise is that the applied system is what the user is really interested in, not just the hardware and the system software. If this applied system is going to be of maximum value to the user, it must be structured in a way that simplifies his total problem, and it must be flexible enough to meet his fundamental wants and needs during its useful lifetime. We have developed an approach to doing just this we call Applied System Architecture. This may be a new expression to many of you, but I'm sure you will be hearing it more in the future.

Now, what do I mean by Applied System Architecture? First, it is a structure that shows how the application, the system software, and the hardware all work together to get the user's job done. Second, it is a building plan for the user to get his applied system from where it is today—from small applications—to total integrated systems. There is a set of techniques for system design, programming, documentation that allows the user to design his application with device independence. Applied System Architecture recognizes that user applications deal with jobs, programs, records, and messages whether they be oriented toward engineering, scientific, or business problems. He would like to design and implement his system in such a way that he is unaware of hardware constraints like bit, byte, words, blocks, sectors, tracks, cylinders, and all the other constraints we hear about. He would like to have the system software efficiently match the application to the hardware without his people all having to be expert computer engineers.

The ability to grow with confidence is one of the most important wants the user has. It is particularly important at this time because, in the next two years, we will see a great change in the user's way of applying computer equipment. The user will need to combine his present way of doing business with a gradual evolution to the new concepts. For example, he will need the ability to perform data input and output both locally and remotely. He will need the ability to organize his data files both sequentially and randomly, with a gradual evolution toward the latter. He will need the ability to process data in batches as well as the ability to process some data incrementally or one transaction at a time. Likewise, he will need the ability to organize his computing facilities both centrally and in a decentralized fashion depending on what is economical for his business at that particular time. He will need to take his single-application files and move toward integrated files. The user must make these choices. The manufacturer should not make the mistake of forcing him into either doing nothing or revolutionizing his way of doing business. The transition should be by evolution, from where he is now to where he wants to go at a speed consistent with his wants, his needs, and his capability. He can only do so if the system architecture permits and encourages him so to do. Given this background of needs, I would like to concentrate on building blocks that appear in an applied system: the message, the program, data base, and the hardware—all of which exist in ever changing combinations. I especially want to discuss how they are controlled or managed in carrying out their intended purpose with what the human mind considers a blinding speed. The formal title of my paper is "Data Base Management: The Keystone of Applied System Architecture." I have chosen the word "keystone" carefully because data base management is an extremely important area. We all know that in a bridge the arches are built of many stones and that they must all stay in place or the bridge will fail. In the same manner applied systems must have more than a good data base management system if they are to succeed. I will concentrate on the total system. So "Data Base Management: The Keystone of Applied System Architecture" with a subtitle "Don't Forget Message Management, Job Management, Computer Program Management, and Media Management" is what we have. I want to start putting these pieces together, the messages, the jobs, programs, data base records, and the media. Let's first examine messages. These are the things that flow through an information system, in contrast to data base records which have a static come-and-get-me-when-you-want-me kind of attitude. They are the real I/O of the system. Let's begin by talking about a message in some detail. We start in the most conventional sense with a message in a letter which is something that a person writes, puts together, and mails to some other person. When we begin to enter the automated world (maybe the U.S. Post Office isn't our carrier), we have a number of administrative message systems backed up by computer. A person at one location can enter information. This message is carried by the system to some other location and delivered to another person. This is the basic concept of a message: the content is known only to the source and destination, and all the other facilities in between are just there to support its transmittal.

Now if we look at the broader general capabilities of our message handling system, we have the ability to send one message to multiple destinations, much in the same way as your secretary may type a letter to Mr. Jones with copies to several other people. Looking at another aspect, we think of a message frequently as being something which stimulates action, giving an instruction, an order for a product, or some other stimulus for action. This is also true when the message is flowing from the external world into the computer and triggers computer processing. I use the word *job* for the element of work being done within the computer, although there are other names in use also, such as task or activity. This job is stimulated by a message, which for instance consists of a stack of punched cards, possibly containing the program deck in binary form as well as the data cards. This is a message, signaling that something is to be done and frequently carrying data to be used during the job execution. Now we see the evolution of the entry point for a message. It no longer needs to be entered through an on-line card reader; the card reader can be remote from the computer. But it is even more interesting to consider input devices that can be operated directly by anyone: teletype machines, display devices with typing capability, and so on. Essentially in this world messages flow from the person, the external world, to the computer to do an automated job. There may be a store-and-forward function involved because of resource scheduling, but I prefer to consider this as being of no direct concern to the user. He should not have to worry about problems like buffering so long as the job gets done within his planned response.

A job also can generate messages. Certainly responses to an inquiry or a report generated on the high-speed printer are messages going back to someone doing a job in the external world. Carrying this thought a step further, we find that jobs not only generate messages to the external world but they also can generate messages to other jobs saying "please do this." One of the most interesting situations in the computer world today is that very few of our very intelligent and capable operating systems allow a job in execution to make a decision as to whether or not to run another job. We think of computers as decision makers, and we let them decide the content of a report; but traditionally, we have not allowed jobs to call out other jobs. We require an operator to do that.

Messages are of three kinds. First is the "action" message—the one that really stimulates jobs. We have a second kind called the "passive" message which is one that comes in and waits for a job to come looking for it. For example, if you have an inventory system that doesn't require updating until night, the inventory messages received during the day are collected until evening when someone triggers a job which comes and looks for them. The third kind of message is a combination active/passive message, called a "hybrid," which is half of one and half of the other. An incoming hybrid message acts like an active message if there is no other such hybrid message already in the system. If there is another hybrid message of the same type, the new one acts as if it were passive. Someone's already stimulated the job.

We have looked at the interaction between a message and a job. We discussed the fact that these jobs are stimulated by, and come into execution because of, a message. Let's now look at the interaction between jobs and the data base and distinguish between data management and data *base* management. Messages are data. Programs are data. All data base records are data. I would like to focus specifically on data base records. Data base records have certain features that make them a property of the applied system; a certain discipline is applied so that many different programs can look at them. They are knowable to many people. This is a characteristic that differentiates data base records from messages. A message only needs to be knowable by the sender and receiver. We can speak in any language as long as the person speaking and the person listening comprehend that language. If we dig into the data base world for a moment, especially data bases of corporate information (corporate meaning a large body, whether it is a business organization, a service organization, a public, educational, or military organization), there is one thing we must recognize. That is the fact that once we go beyond the capability of one man, what he can do with his hands and with his own mind, then the exchange of information between people begins. The effectiveness of a large corporation and the ultimate limit to its size depend on how well it can store and process the data relevant to its operations and how well it can communicate between its components. The real data base of an organization is large. I don't know what large really means, but it is not 10 million or 20 million characters; 10 billion characters is more like it. This quantity at the moment is almost incomprehensible, yet we have the technical capability today to process that amount of data and we have the hardware to support it. But I am not sure whether we have the management organization capability to collect the data, support it, or train the people to use it properly. We also have the problem of data organization, both in terms of records, fields, chains, sets, indexes, etc, and, in another aspect, problems in terms of media organization. Here we need a bridge between the hardware, bits, bytes, tapes, disks, and the user. We need procedural statements so that we have some way of talking to the data base. We already have well developed languages, such as the GE Integrated Data Store with statements like STORE, RETRIEVE, MODIFY, and DELETE. G.M.'s Associative Programming Language uses FIND instead of RETRIEVE and CREATE instead of STORE. But the words themselves are not important. It is the functions that must be there. Furthermore, data declarations defining fields, records, and chains are necessary. Data protection functions are also very important because the data base is, in effect, the foundation on which a business operates. Not the only foundation, but if a data base were destroyed, there could be a crisis. If one wiped out a business's set of orders or an airline's reservations, you could imagine the chaos that would be created. Such a data base must be protected against many kinds of hazards. We must worry about the thief. Someone might want to steal competitive information like the open orders. Noncompetitive information, like salaries, is often considered to be confidential, needing some kind of lock. We certainly need protection of some kind on profits, budgets, and similar data. Many existing systems have the ability to lock out a file, but as we move toward integrated files, the user won't want to lock out an entire file or an entire record. For example, he may want to take a personnel record and lock out the man's salary, leaving his name, address and telephone, or current work assignment as completely free and available information. So we need security locks at the field level.

A completely different kind of security problem is that of interaction between programs that run together. Just think of a freeway at rush hour, with 20 or 30 or 50 cars being driven one car length apart at 70 miles an hour, every driver hoping that nothing up front will happen. Having separate lanes helps somewhat. Looking now at all foreseeable mass storage hardware, we will still have a limitation in terms of turnaround time to handle all requests of information in a sequential manner. Most of today's mass storage devices offer parallelism as an opportunity for getting greater throughput. In a sense this is what's happening on the expressway. In data base management then we have the problem of protecting the files from collision. One of the easiest solutions is uniprogramming. I think this is the area in which we have most experience, but I'm afraid that this nice, simple solution is almost gone. Once we venture into multiprogramming, in order to get more throughput or to get response from program A while program B is still running, we find only two choices allowed to us. One is the concept I call declared isolation, where someone says, "I want data base A to be reserved for me." This concept is applicable to a partial data base, like the part with all manufacturing information or the part with all personnel information, where the user program requests isolation of the manufacturing information while instructing the operating system to stop all other programs from accessing this part of the data base. This is good if you are not really serious about automated data base management or about the ability to do a lot of processing. However, if you contemplate a system that might have as many as ten jobs running simultaneously, all doing order processing and maybe all doing order processing for the same inventory item of the same warehouse, then you have to have a better isolation mechanism than subfile declarations. At this point you need an access-time isolation where each user gets access to what he asks for but is delayed if the data he desires is currently isolated by another job. This lock can be operative at either the page level or the record level. So in a sense, we have a traffic cop situation. This may, at first glance, look like a very old-fashioned way of handling data traffic, but it is very practical if you can provide the traffic cop efficiently and economically.

In order to make a job run we need a procedure. A procedure within a computer is typically called a computer program. We also need some hardware in order to run this thing, some space in core memory, also a processor, something which can do the manipulation of the program. We need channels to be allocated from time to time so that data can flow through them. We are also going to look at the data base. The data base is interacting with the job, putting in its input. We look at the output briefly and see that we can also generate many messages, or even programs, if the job that is running happens to be a compilation. It also may, from time to time, release the hardware if it is no longer in use; it may update the data base. Now, if we look at all these things together, job control interacts with the four major subsystems, data base management, message management, program management, and hardware management.

In addition to these functions, there are two major problem areas that a viable information system must be capable of handling. These are job scheduling and recovery and restart.

Job scheduling essentially is the resolution of conflicts arising from fluctuating demands placed against constant resources. So long as these demands don't exceed the capacity of available resources, no arbitration needs to take place. In times of peak demands, however, when demands placed on the system exceed capacity, it becomes necessary to allocate which jobs will be processed, to what extent, and which ones will be temporarily put on a waiting list. The first-come-first-served scheduling system has been quite useful in the past, but it is rapidly becoming obsolete. Chronological order alone is an insufficient criterion for assignment of resources. "All share alike" is a nice principle but a very unrealistic scheduling algorithm. There are two elements that are essential to a practical job scheduling system; namely, job priority and required response time. Without this knowledge, no intelligent scheduling can take place.

Recovery and restart procedures traditionally attempt to minimize time losses resulting from media failure, application failure, or system failure. As systems are becoming increasingly complex, more and more things can go wrong with them; and consequently, recovery and restart has to recognize and handle a large variety of problems.

Application failure in a multiprogramming environment could conceivably affect other concurrently running programs. The situation becomes even worse when several jobs share the data base. Mutual job interlocks have to be recognized and prevented. The effects of a failed program on the shared data base have to be pinpointed and, if necessary, removed.

Data base restructuring systems are essential to evolutionary requirements. People must be given a chance to experiment, make mistakes at times, without being penalized for attempting to progress. This freedom to experiment is hardly possible when facilities of erasing the effects of a trial from the data base are not readily available.

In summary, I would like to quote Peter Drucker: "The role of a business is to create a customer." I predict that the manufacturer in our industry who develops and exploits an Applied System Architecture responsive to the users' desires for change, tempered with a step-by-step implementation technique, will create an even bigger market than we can envision today. It is important that the Information Systems industry make the same kind of breakthrough that the automobile industry experienced when General Motors offered its customers a choice—in contrast with Henry Ford's attitude, "You can have any color you want, as long as it's black!" Applied systems, capable of responding to users' desires and choices, will signal the end of the "Model T" computer era.

Survey of Management Information Systems

and Their Languages

J. FRY
J. GOSDEN

Mitre Corporation
Washington, D.C.

1. INTRODUCTION

In this short paper it is not possible to do justice to the variety of data management systems that are available or imminent. Rather, this paper presents an overview of several major data management systems selected as typical in three categories of user languages. A survey of the detailed characteristics (languages, data structures, and facilities) of some dozen systems is presented in another paper. [1] That paper is a formal, organized, and consistent tabular restatement of the claimed characteristics of the data management systems and does not represent an evaluation.

Other writers have discussed the characteristics and properties of other systems, but we particularly recommend the articles by Canning [2, 3] as fine descriptive reports on current systems. We are also assuming that our audience is generally familiar with data management systems and the important data structure concepts being developed. For a general reference manual offering extensive bibliographies and first-class reviews rather than opinions, we recommend the American Documentation Institute's Annual Reviews. [4]

It is interesting that the major thrust of the development of data management systems has not come from the hardware manufacturers, but rather from military command and control systems and user groups. Indeed the trend has continued so that now the software houses are making major contributions in this area, and we have selected most of our examples from that source.

Data management systems are really an outgrowth from report program generators (RPGs). Thus one of the early ancestors was the set of report generators produced for the IBM 702. The first of these, the MARK I Generalized Report Generator, was completed about 1956, and the second, the MARK II Generalized Report and File Maintenance Generator, was a 1957 vintage system. This was followed later by 9PAC on the IBM 709 and 7090 in 1958-1959, while at about the same time the TUFF-TUG-IRS implementation on the 704 began the series of military data management systems (sometimes called command and control systems) that has led to FFS and NIPS, which in turn seem to be the immediate ancestors of Generalized Information System (GIS) being developed by IBM. Meanwhile, 9PAC has been the main ancestor for most nonmilitary implementations.

2. MAJOR CLASSES OF LANGUAGE

In general the scope of capabilities provided in major data management systems does not vary very much. The major differences lie in the form of the user languages, which are the user interface to the system. Such languages cover several major functional areas:

> Describing data
> Input
> Update
> reorganization
> Retrieval
> Sorting
> Presentation

The general user is most concerned with queries to a data base that utilize the last three areas. In many cases sorting and presentation are automatic or separate functions and the major language differences are typified by the languages used to define the retrieval required.

Retrieval languages divide into three major categories:

> own Data Management Language (DML)
> forms controlled
> Procedure Oriented Language (POL) Embedded

The three categories can be briefly contrasted as follows: Own DML Systems are imitative of conventional POL's; Forms Controlled Systems use well tried "forms" techniques common in everyday business and public life; and POL Embedded Systems take advantage of existing powerful programming languages.

3. OWN DML SYSTEMS

These systems are imitative of POLs. They used the style and approach of POLs but used a new format and verbs specifically developed for data management. Just as FORTRAN was oriented toward scientific computation and COBOL toward business needs, so DMLs were oriented toward data management. They followed the example of COBOL in separating the input for various functional areas, e.g., data description, retrieval conditions, and output format. Indeed, they developed separate languages for each functional area, taking advantage of the fact that different kinds of users are involved. For example, data description languages for systems specialists to establish the file structure, maintenance languages for clerks who nurture the data base, and query languages for casual users. They also simplified the programming skills needed, first by restricting themselves to basic functions such as sum, count, and average, and second by eliminating many housekeeping chores, especially I/O control, and also the specific counting through records, repeated sets, and individual fields. In fact some parts of DMLs, especially query languages, are problem oriented languages, a specialized type of POL. They are used to specify what is to be done, not how it is to be done. In particular, most query languages are content oriented. They provide content retrieval; e.g., what is the division of the man whose name is G. Parker? The NIPS and TDMS systems described below are typical members of this category.

NATIONAL MILITARY COMMAND SYSTEM/NIPS

Background. The NMCS Information Processing System (NIPS/360) is in essence the Formatted File System (FFS) converted to the IBM 360/50 computer system and operational under Operating System 360/Option 2. Historically, the FFSs began with the SAC 438L system on the IBM 7090 in 1961. The NIPS predecessor on the IBM 1410 was created in 1963 to satisfy the mission of a Naval Fleet Intelligence Center. Since then the system has been employed at several intelligence centers and commands throughout the world. Basically, the system has evolved in two separate communities: Command and Control, and Intelligence. The Intelligence system (IDHS FFS) has emphasized efficient processing capabilities and improved output options for their many volumed data sources. On the other hand, the Command and Control system (NIPS) has expanded logical file maintenance, improved the query language, and built an on-line retrieval mechanism. Both the second-generation FFS systems operate under the modified 1410 operating system OPSYS (1410-PR-155).

The 1410 FFS is being converted to an S/360 model 50H (eight magnetic tape drives, two 2311 discs, one 2394 disc, 2260/1053, and associated card/

read/punch printer equipment) in two primary phases. Phase I components include file structuring, file maintenance, retrieval and sort, output, remote inquiry processing, system formatted output, and necessary utilities. Included in Phase II are expanded file maintenance including multifile capabilities, file revision, on-line update, as well as additional components and utilities. The target date for the operational capabilities was January 1968, for Phase I and June 1968, for Phase II.

Summary of Capabilities.   NIPS/360 is a general-purpose file handling system operating under O/S 360 and performing the traditional functions of structuring, maintaining, revising, and retrieving from a set of data files. While maintaining a high degree of external compatibility with its 1410 predecessor, the internal processing methods have been modified to exploit the capabilities of the third-generation hardware S/360 and of operating system O/S 360. Adhering to the strict O/S 360 programming conventions for communication, base register usage, linkage, etc., the conversion is being done using the COBOL language down to the subroutine level of software. At the subroutine level, either COBOL or assembly language will be used depending on which is necessary to efficiently utilize O/S 360 software and S/360 hardware capabilities.

Compatibility with the existing 1410 FFS system was a major design criterion which is being achieved through the ability to use existing FFS control cards, query and summary decks, file maintenance decks, and analyst's procedures.

Specific Features.   The new system does much to alleviate the physical restrictions of the old system. Specifically, the physical size restriction of a logical record to 2701 characters has been relieved by making each individual group instance a physical record. However, because of compatibility requirements, some of the logical shortcomings are still apparent in the system.

In the new system, each File Format Table (FFT is the computer form of the data description or dictionary) will be stored with its file. Thus the NIPS files will be "self-describing" and no longer have a physical remote file description which can easily be misplaced or lost. This should be a major factor in making the transfer of data possible among various installations and is an important development. The S/360 NIPS is primarily a direct access oriented system utilizing the capabilities of the disk through the Index Sequential Access Method (ISAM) of O/S 360.

The query language for NIPS, called RASP (Retrieval and Sort Processor) is a good example of its kind. Figure 1 shows the rules for the IF clause which illustrates the POL-like structure and the wide variety of alternatives possible.

IF FIELD EQUALS VALUE

CONNECTOR	FIELD	OPERATOR	DATA BASE VALUE	
IF	FFT	EQ EQUAL	$	ANY VALUE
AND	OR GROUP	EQA EQUAL α	—	BLANK
OR	NAME	EQN EQUAL N	+ FIELD	FILE FIELD NAME
		LT LESS THAN	VALUE	VALUE
		LTA LESS THAN α	==VALUE #	CANCELS SUB
		LTN LESS THAN N		CONVERSION

Fig. 1 NIPS "IF" STATEMENT

SYSTEM DEVELOPMENT CORPORATION/TDMS

Background. The Time-Shared Data Management System (TDMS) is a general-purpose system for managing data in a time-sharing environment. It is currently being developed by the Technology Directorate of the System Development Corporation (SDC) as a result of work sponsored in part by the Advanced Research Projects Agency (ARPA) of the Department of Defense. TDMS is being designed and implemented for use on the IBM System 360 Model 50. TDMS is an outgrowth of TSS-Lucid System also developed by SDC for the AN/FSQ-32 computer.

Summary of Capabilities. TDMS will permit the user to describe and generate a file as well as retrieve and display data from the file on a cathode-ray tube (CRT) device. It also will provide the capabilities to up-date and maintain the file and to generate hard copy reports. TDMS operates under the SDC-provided ADEPT operating system. ADEPT provides a time-sharing environment that we define as an environment having on-line access and multiple access and rapid response.

Specific Features. To achieve rapid response in any large data base it is necessary to be able to provide an access mechanism based on content. Inverted files or indexes and associative memories are two techniques used to do this. TDMS uses a type of inverted file.

In TDMS a file is stored in a series of associated tables. One group of tables holds the actual data element values. There is a separate table for each defined data element, and only unique data element values are stored in these tables (i.e., no duplicate values). Another table contains the names of the data elements in the files. A third type of table describes the individual data elements and their logical relationships. It also points to tables that contain pointers arranged in sorted order, which point to the tables containing the actual data element values.

This system provides a variety of on-line services oriented to users who are not programmers.

There are two capabilities in TDMS that can be used to retrieve data. One of these, QUERY, can produce only relatively simple outputs. A typical example is "PRINT JOB TITLE WHERE POSITION EQUALS PROJECT HEAD." The second, COMPOSE/PRODUCE, can produce rather sophisticated outputs. Within COMPOSE, the user describes any number of report formats to TDMS. Each report format has a name and requires several statements to describe the data that is to be output and the way the output will look when it has been produced as a report. PRODUCE provides the user with the capability of requesting any of the report formats previously generated in COMPOSE to produce actual reports.

Through two additional programs TDMS has capabilities for modifying data element values and for maintaining files. The UPDATE program allows the user to add, delete, or change data element values. The MAINTAIN program provides for merging, subsetting, extracting, ordering, and restructuring of files.

4. FORMS CONTROLLED SYSTEMS

These systems are dominated by a design goal to provide a simple-to-use interface. Well-designed forms can contain self-explanatory user instructions, reduce the human input, and thus reduce errors in language use and input to the system. This is possible because data management systems do not need all of the facilities of a POL. As the variety of facilities in such systems has increased, so the number of forms needed has increased. The COGENT and MARK IV systems described below are typical members of this category.

It is interesting to note that there is a very strong relation between forms controlled languages and interactive on-line query languages. For every box on a form there is a preprinted question or instruction to the user, and the user enters his response. Sometimes the response is made easy by a multiple-choice format. Most interactive query languages use the same technique presenting one box at a time to the user who enters his response. In online mode the housekeeping actions such as "If you answer yes to question 7, ignore questions 8 and 9, and go to question 10" is automated. Thus simple forms controlled systems should be easy to convert to on-line.

The two systems described below also typify the advent of software houses providing off-the-shelf generalized software packages. In order to appeal to a wide market, they have extended forms control to include own-code, usually in a conventional POL, and have made provisions to accept files and data descriptions directly from other POLs. Thus we begin to see the merging of all three types of retrieval language that we identified earlier: Own DML, Forms Controlled, and POL Embedded.

COMPUTER SCIENCES CORPORATION/COGENT III

Background. COGENT III, a COBOL-compatible generalized file management system, is an advanced general-purpose data management system developed by Computer Sciences Corporation (CSC) for the IBM/360 family of equipment. COGENT III represents the next development in a series of generalized file management systems produced by CSC. It follows COGENT II, also developed for the IBM/360 family, a series of COGENT systems developed for the IBM 7090, UNIVAC 1107/1108, IBM 7044, and RCA SPECTRA 70.

COGENT III is modular in construction and is designed to function on a wide range of System/360 configurations. It provides for use of unit record, magnetic tape, and direct access devices, as well as teleprocessing equipment. The system employs and is compatible with O/S 360 and the related COBOL compiler.

Summary of Capabilities.   COGENT III generalizes the major data processing functions associated with information storage, maintenance, retrieval, and presentation. The system allows for use of a common data base by various groups of users. This facility is provided under the control of a single, comprehensive data directory that describes all data used or referenced by the system, as well as describing the relationships between data sets, records, and data fields in the data base.

COGENT III consists of an information system language and a language processor (implemented in COBOL) that interprets this language and generates functional COBOL programs for maximum machine independence to perform the information system tasks requested. In addition an interactive inquiry retrieval and storage language is provided to meet rapid response requirements. This language is processed by the COGENT III Interpretive Processor which is implemented in assembly language employing re-entrant code. The system provides for specification and generation of program(s) for a simple function, an entire data processing application, and/or a series of integrated applications in addition to interpretive processing of dynamic requests for information storage and retrieval including on-line data input.

Specific Capabilities.   The information system language consists of fixed-form data descriptions and functional specifications as well as an interactive inquiry and storage language. The language elements are designed to allow specification of the information needs of information collection, storage, maintenance, retrieval, and presentation for various levels of users, such as management, operating personnel, and system analysts.

In general the language allows the user to specify the following:

1. information to be stored in the data base
2. source of the information
3. how and under what conditions the information is created and maintained
4. what relationships exist between different collections of information (hierarchical structure and integration between data sets)
5. who can have access to modify or retrieve the information
6. how and under what conditions the information is to be retrieved
7. how the information is to be presented
8. on-line, off-line, batched, real-time or demand processing of tasks

The Data Descriptions allow the user to describe such items as data fields, relationships between data fields, security codes for maintenance and retrieval, decoding and encoding association tables, physical characteristics of data elements, and presentation format of data elements, which fields may be used as access keys for content retrieval, and which fields are record identifiers.

The Functional Specifications allow the user to specify

1. the task control information for creation, maintenance, sorting, and reporting
2. the processing mode—direct, demand, or batch
3. the file structure—serial or direct

The interactive inquiry retrieval and storage language allows the user to access the data base via ad hoc queries and execution of previously defined queries. The user can obtain immediate response or can batch queries.

Hierarchical data structures are provided on both serial, direct access data sets as well as between multiple data sets. In most cases, hierarchical records physically follow their associated higher level records. In the case of multiple data sets, different levels of hierarchical records may be physically stored on different devices (direct access only).

When stored on direct access devices, the record keys as defined by the Data Description language are employed to build a record key index. This is one method of content access used to provide rapid response. Records are indexed by hierarchical group only. Individual records within the hierarchy are extracted in core from physical blocks containing a hierarchical group.

An Access Key index is automatically constructed for each data field defined as an access field in the Data Description language The index contains an entry for each possible field value with pointers (record key) to all physical blocks that contain the value. This is a selective form of content access.

INFORMATICS/MARK IV

Background.   The MARK IV file management system is an advanced general-purpose software system developed for the IBM/360 series of equipment. It is the fifth in a series of data management systems designed and developed by Informatics. MARK IV operates under either the Standard Disk Operating System (DOS) or Operating System (OS). The initial system was available during the latter part of 1967 and a final version early in 1968.

Summary of Capabilities.   MARK IV is a data processing system designed primarily for business or file applications. The system provides for the generation, maintenance, and retrieval of information from tape or disk oriented files. A comprehensive report facility is also provided.

The system generates computer programs based upon specifications given to it by the user. The user employs one or more structured forms to prepare the specifications that become the MARK IV source input. No on-line facilities are now provided by the system.

Specific Features.   MARK IV generates a program to perform the user-specified functions from precoded routines stored in the MARK IV library. The precoded routines provide for many of the common data processing tasks, thus reducing the amount of code that has to be generated.

The user specifies the logical organization of his files, and the data are stored on tapes or on disk. The data are accessed via the Sequential Access Method (SAM) if the storage medium is tapes, and by the SAM or the Index Sequential Access Method (ISAM) if the storage medium is disk.

The system can create files from various data sources; maintain files by performing changes, additions, and deletions; select data records based on selected criteria; make computations on the data in these records; extract data items from selected records; and produce new files, parts of files, and combinations of files. Various report formats and data arrangements, as well as the facility to use preprinted forms, are available.

In addition to the standard set of programs provided by MARK IV, the user also is provided with the facility for calling up user-coded routines, "own-code," which may be required for special processing. The system also has the facility for saving a generated program in its library and calling upon the program if the user results are required on a periodic basis.

5. POL EMBEDDED SYSTEMS

These systems, instead of inventing new languages, have utilized and extended existing POLs, mainly COBOL and recently PL/1. Therefore, they provide all the power of a POL without the need for special linkages. The IDS, ICS (an expansion of DL-1), and DM-1 systems described below are typical but surprisingly different members of this category.

GENERAL ELECTRIC/IDS

Background.   Integrated Data Store (IDS) is a data management system designed and developed by the General Electric Company in 1965. It has been implemented in the GE200, 400, and 600 series of computers.

Summary of Capabilities.   IDS, in concert with COBOL, provides the capability for generating, maintaining, and retrieving data from disk resident files. IDS operates under the control of the GE multiprogramming monitor, which provides an on-line remote terminal inquiry capability.

Specific Features.   IDS is embedded in COBOL. All the features available in COBOL are available to the IDS user. Some of the COBOL procedures statements have been modified, and other statements have been added to the basic language in order to accommodate IDS structured files. All maintenance, retrieval, and outputting is accomplished by using COBOL. Theoretically, a distinct set of procedures, a unique COBOL program, might be required for each type of update or query.

IDS provides the facility for placing data in the file and retrieving from it. The functions performed by IDS itself can be likened to that of special input and output subroutines.

A variety of physical and logical file structures are possible under IDS. The user has the traditional capability of specifying the logical structure of his data; he also has some control over the physical structure. IDS provides the capability of linking together any combinations of master or repeating groups to form an entry. During file maintenance linkages are changed to reflect any additions or deletions to the file. Neither groups nor entries need to be physically stored sequentially. They may be stored in a random order, since the links connect all the groups constituting an entry and an entry is randomized on its key element(s).

IDS pioneered the use of the notion of "sets" typified by list-processing and ring structures. This is a powerful data structure concept; hierarchies can be represented in it but it cannot be represented in physical hierarchical structures. This kind of power is becoming more important as we begin to implement integrated data bases and was essential to the effective development of on-line graphics as exemplified in Sketchpad. [5]

IDS on the GE400 and 600 series of computers operates under the multiprogramming monitor and functions like any other processor (e.g., FORTRAN) in the environment.

There are other basic differences in the versions of IDS available on the GE200, 400, and 600 series. The 200 series does not use COBOL, but an assembly language. The differences between the 400 and 600 series are less pronounced, but they do exist primarily in the COBOL language modifications and additions.

NORTH AMERICAN AVIATION/DL-1

Background.   Data Language-1 (DL-1) is a data management system devloped jointly by the Space Division of North American Aviation, Inc. (NAA) and International Business Machines Corporation (IBM) in 1966.

The DL-1 effort is a continuing joint effort by IBM and NAA based on their previous experience with a system called DATE, which was implemented on the IBM 7010 computer. The first version of DL-1 will contain all the features of 7010 DATE system. DL-1 is written for the IBM 360 family of computers and requires Operating System/360 and Data Management to operate. The system also uses COBOL and PL/I as programming languages.

An on-line facility, called Information Control System (ICS), has also been planned. This system interfaces with DL-1 and permits simultaneous execution of teleprocessing and conventional batch processing programs. ICS includes a routine to handle 60 remote terminals and 50 different types of messages. The system operates under the OS/360 Interim Sequential Partitioned System, and was implemented during the early part of 1968.

Summary of Capabilities.   DL-1 provides a user with the means to organize and describe a hierarchically structured data base. The system creates a set of directories and data description tables required when the data base is initially loaded into the system and when the data is retrieved and manipulated during the execution of the user's applications programs. Data base definition is external to the applications program. DL-1 also provides the means for applications programs to interface with the system in order to create, maintain, and retrieve data from the data base. The system also allows for more than one applications program to access the same data base and allows logical records to span one or more physical disk tracks if necessary.

Storage media for the data base can be either tapes or disks. The data in tape files are accessed by the Sequential Access Method (SAM) while disk files are accessed via the Index Sequential Access Method (ISAM).

Specific Features.   DL-1 is an interface between problem oriented compilers (COBOL and PL/I) and the IBM operating system OS/360. The primary point of contact of DL-1 with OS/360 is the Data Management section of OS/360, which is an I/O system that provides such data handling services as buffering and storage device control.

The system does not have its own retrieval languages. Each user of the data base is required to prepare an applications program in COBOL or PL/I in order to manipulate the data base. The applications programs contain interface statements to the PL/I system and a communications table called a Program Communication Block (PCB). The interface statements consist of COBOL or PL/I "calls" to DL-1 followed by a series of parameters that indicate the type of operation on the data base that is desired. The actual operation on the data base will be performed by the DL-1 system.

An output formatting program is not available in the first version of the system but is being planned for future versions. Theoretically, this facility could be provided by a COBOL or PL/I applications program.

This system also incorporates strong separate terminal and data file protection.

AUERBACH/DM-1

Background.   Data Manager-1 (DM-1) is a generalized data management software system designed by Auerbach Corporation as a proprietary package. The system is being implemented on two distinctly different hardware systems: on a Univac 1218 (Mil Spec 418) for the U.S. Air Force under contract through the Rome Air Development Center and on the IBM 360/50 for the Western Electric Corporation.

Summary of Capabilities.   The DM-1 system provides program and job library services, data storage and access services, and job execution control. The job library contains a number of general-purpose system jobs for building, maintaining, and querying the data base and job library. User jobs can be added to this library. The structure of the data pool provides logically for definition of items and defines a structure for a set of directory tables.

Basically DM-1 provides a nucleus system with emphasis on data definition, data structuring, and data access methods. Features such as generalized report generators, user query and maintenance languages, and recording services are not defined in the DM-1 design. It is intended that these items be developed for each customer as separate units to be integrated into the system, and currently COBOL can be used as a retrieval language. Programs (generalized report generators) would be added to the job library with no unique status. The syntax of system languages (query, maintenance) can be defined by the user through a meta language (similar to ALGOL).

Specific Features.   DM-1 has been designed independently of a specific computer: however, the system is designed to utilize fully the capabilities of whatever operating system that DM-1 is to run under. A standard interface is provided to the computer through the use of the data service routines, which are theoretically the only computer dependent routines of the system.

DM-1 has a very comprehensive logical file structuring capability. The system has been designed to provide a very powerful data structure facility that can provide complex hierarchies of logical relationships in the form of general linked-tree structures. The data description language permits the use of variable length data elements, optional data elements, and nested structures.

The DM-1 data pool is a series of fixed length data segments containing an unformatted stream of bits. The segment size of the data pool is independent of the logical file organization and theoretically utilizes the maximum buffer size of the operating system. The DM-1 access mechanism, which utilizes the IOCS, transfers the data between the data pool and core. The segmented data stream is interpreted in core by the data service routines with the aid of the system directories and the segment index.

REFERENCES

1. The MITRE Corporation, "A Survey of Data Management Systems," MTR-5036, March 7, 1968.

2. *EDP Analyzer*, V, No. 12 (December 1967), Canning Publications, Inc., Vista, California.

3. *EDP Analyzer*, VI, No.1 (January 1968), Canning Publications, Inc., Vista, Calif.

4. American Documentation Institute, *Annual Review of Information Science and Technology*, ed. Carlos A. Cuadra. New York: Interscience Publishers, 1967.

5. SUTHERLAND, I. E., "Sketchpad: A Man-Machine Graphical Communication System," *AFIPS Conf. Proc.*, XXIII, 1963 Spring Joint Computer Conference.

BIBLIOGRAPHY

BACHMAN, C. W., "Software for Random Access Processing," *Datamation* (April 1965).

BACHMAN, C. W., and S. B. WILLIAMS, "A General Purpose Programming System for Random Access Memories," *Proc. of the FJCC*, XXVI (1964).

BLEIER, R. E., "Treating Hierarchical Structures in the SDC Time-Shared Data Management System (TDMS)," SP 2750, 20 August 1967.

Computer Sciences Corporation, "COGENT II Specifications," 1967.

Computer Sciences Corporation, "Introduction to COGENT II," 1967.

Defense Intelligence Agency, "IDHS 1410 Formatted File System: Programming Maintenance Manual," Washington, D. C., 20 January 1967 (DIAM–65–9–4) (AD 648 020).

Defense Intelligence Agency, "IDHS 1410 Formatted File System: File Maintenance and File Generation Manual" (rev. ed.), Washington, D. C., 1 August 1966 (DIAM–65–9–1) (AD 637 018).

Defense Intelligence Agency, "IDHS 1410 Formatted File System: Retrieval and Output Manual" (rev. ed.), Washington, D. C., 1 August 1966 (DIAM–65–9–2) (AD 637 018).

Defense Intelligence Agency, "IDHS 1410 Formatted File System Operator's Manual," Washington D. C., 1 January 1966 (DIAM–65–9–3) (AD 637 019).

FRANKS, E. W., "A Data Management System for Time-Shared File Processing Using a Cross-Index File and Self-Defined Entries," *Proc. SJCC*, XXVIII (1966).

General Electric, "Integrated Data Store," CPB-483 (5C 10–16).

General Electric, "Introduction to Integrated Data Store," CPB-1048, April 1965.

North American Aviation, Inc., and IBM, Data Language No. 1 (DL-1) Encyclopedia, Publication 2541-F, April 1967.

North American Aviation, Inc., and IBM, ICS: Information Control System.

POSTLEY, J. A., "Informatics MARK IV File Management System: Summary of Characteristics," AIS 66–016.

POSTLEY, J. A., "MARK IV System," *Datamation* (January 1968).

RAUNCHER, V., and H. S. SCHWIMMER, "The Basic Language Specification of TDMS, Phase II: Report Production," System Development Corporation, TM-3370/008/00.

RAUNCHER, V., "The Language Specifications for the Query Operation of TDMS," System Development Corporation, TM-3370/004/00.

RAUNCHER, V., "The Language Specifications for the Update Operation of TDMS," System Development Corporation, TM-3370/005/00.

REYNOLDS, J. D., N. BOSAK, and J. R. SHIBAN, "The Language Specifications for the Load Operation of TDMS," System Development Corporation, TM-3370/007/00.

SABLE, J., et al., "Design of Reliability Central Data Management Subsystem," Final report, Auerbach Corporation, Philadelphia, Pa., July 1965, Vol. 2, RADC TR–65–189–Vol. 2 (AD 469 269).

SABLE, J., W. CROWLEY, M. ROSENTHAL, S. FORST, and P. HARPER, "Reliability Central Automatic Data Processing Subsystem," Vol. 1 Design Specification Report. Final report, Auerbach Corp., Philadelphia, Pa., August 1966 (Report no. 1280–TR–Vol. 1), RADC TR–66–474–Vol. 1.

SABLE, J., W. CROWLEY, M. ROSENTHAL, S. FORST, and P. HARPER, "Reliability Central Automatic Data Processing Subsystem," Vol. 2 Design Specification Report (Cont'd). Final report, Auerbach Corp., Philadelphia, Pa., August 1966 (Report no. 1280–TR–Vol. 2), RADC TR–66–474–Vol. 2 (AD 489 667).

SABLE, J. and J. MINKER, "Reliability Central Automatic Data Processing Subsystem," Vol. 3 Data Management System Survey. Final report, Auerbach Corporation, Philadelphia, Pa., August 1966 (Report no. 1280–TR–Vol. 3), RADC TR–66–474–Vol. 3 (AD 489 668).

Systems Design of a Computer for

Time-sharing Applications: In Hindsight

MELVIN PIRTLE

Associate Professor of Electrical Engineering
University of California, Berkeley

Let me begin by explaining a little about the current situation at Berkeley relative to research in computer systems. First, since our work is mainly supported by ARPA, we feel that we can gamble in trying to advance in fairly large steps. Unfortunately, later reflections on past work frequently reveal that we have advanced only by rather small steps. Second, we have terminated our work on the present time-sharing system—the one which resulted in the SDS 940—and we are currently devoting considerable energy toward the development of a second system.

Before proceeding further, I would like to comment on the term "time-sharing." In the early days of time-sharing we thought we had at least a vague understanding of the meaning of the term. Today, however, it appears that almost anything that has a terminal of any kind attached to it is called a time-sharing system. All I can do is describe what we at Berkeley now think of as a time-sharing system.

Time-sharing to us is a mechanism for providing a wide range of computing services including those generally known as real-time, conversational, and batch processing. Of course, these terms are also not well defined. Let me just indicate that we regard real-time as a service that provides response on the order of 100 to 200 microseconds, and at the other extreme batch processing may have a 12-hour turnaround time. Conversational service encompasses a response time on the order of 1 second and numerous facilities for on-line interaction.

It should be clear that our notion of time-sharing is not the common one in which you have a large number of users essentially baby sitting their tele-types, waiting for 5 or 10 minutes for the terminal to say something, and always afraid to leave it because it might.

Our main goal in developing systems is to maximize the effectiveness of the user. The utility of the hardware and effectiveness of the operating system are subgoals, of course, but are always secondary.

It should also be pointed out that at Berkeley we are pursuing only a small part of the work required to develop a total system. As is pointed out in another presentation, the real difficulties—the real problem areas—lie in the applications of time-sharing. At Berkeley we have tried to develop basic systems of sufficient capability that the users can focus their attentions on applications. In this regard, these systems are designed to be as flexible as we feel is practical. However, we do not attempt to develop application programs except a few for demonstration purposes.

In developing a time-sharing system, we are led immediately to problem areas like interjob communication, the creation and control of jobs and processes —even the definition of what constitutes a job. It is far from clear, in a time-sharing atmosphere, just what a job is. I will refer to an entity that we call a *process*, a program that gets scheduled within the time-sharing system. We think that we understand what we call processes—they have a state vector, they get scheduled, and they are executed. A job is some ill-defined collection of processes.

Another important area is that of input/output. To us, I/O is strictly trans-mission to and from remote terminals; that is, we have no local I/O. We think in terms of hardware that is in a locked room, and someone goes in every month or two to see that it's still running. Traditional I/O devices like card readers and printers will be provided, of course, but they will be remote from the computing facilities and will be treated as any other termi-nal. This philosophy creates some problems but eliminates many more. The virtue to us is a uniform interface for all I/O devices. There is local transfer of information between drums, disks, (possibly) tapes, and the processor; but we place these transfers in a different category.

Another problem area which has been mentioned is that of locking files, or portions of files. Suppose that a low-priority user locks a file, and before he is serviced a high-priority user calls for access to that file. What should the system do? One obvious solution is to raise the priority of the user who locked the file to at least the priority level of the user who wants access. There are many similar situations that require altering priorities dynamically, according to decision processes that involve a large number of factors. Even at that, the adjustment of priorities is only one of many aspects of the problem of locking files.

A paramount problem is reliability. We assume that there will be some hardware problems, a lot more software problems, and that we must be able to recover from all of them. We have had good luck with our hardware and have developed recovery procedures for nearly every situation; unfortunately, they are a bit gross at times. They delete some files, for example, when it really isn't necessary. In the typical case of trouble, we cause some discomfort for one user, but the others carry on with little interruption. The problem of recovery is one of basic design. There must be a lot of redundancy in most tables. We have found the hardware to be much more reliable than the software, and we rely heavily on hardware to assist in the recovery procedures.

Yet another problem is that of resource allocation. Any device that is shared (core, drum, disk, etc.) must be allocated, and the typical user should not be required to be concerned with the allocation mechanism. On the other hand, we feel that any given user might have unusual needs for a resource and therefore should have access to the allocator. His problem may call for an abnormal amount of drum to disk swapping, for example. If this is the case, he should be able to reserve a portion of the device for his use, as well as a period of uninterrupted access (this period of time being on the order of several hundred milliseconds).

Another of our tenets is that the scheduling of user processes should be handled not only on the basis of the priority of the user, but also on the task that the process is to pursue (as determined, for example, by the activation condition), the acceptable response time for this task, and the resources used by this process in the immediate past (of, say, 5 to 10 seconds). Thus, the user should be provided with specified resources and specified response times, where both the character and amount of resources and the response times are functions of the user and the current activity of the process. Furthermore, users should be granted an option of a guaranteed service. There are many applications that are simply not worthwhile unless the users have 8-hour access to the system and some nominal percentage of the CPU guaranteed to them. In real time applications, there must be guarantee also of the proper share of core, drum, and disk storage as needed. Some real time processes must also remain resident in core while being executed.

The biggest problem is to create a tariff structure that will be commensurate with a wide range of services. Without it, there are bound to be abuses, and even with it, it is necessary to have the authority to prevent someone from saturating the entire system for an extended period.

We were fortunate in our work in being able to start from ground zero, as opposed to, "If Manufacturer X makes a computer, how can we make use of it?" Actually, we were rather lazy and preferred to start from scratch and design a total system. With some hardware, a monitor, and a battery of utility routines, we attempt to provide a good interface to the community that would use the system in its final glory. The hard core (monitor) is assumed to be immune to user modification. The utility routines, on the other hand, can be modified by the users, so that they can be tailored by him to his needs.

A user, for example, can modify the file system, or he may create his own. We hope that many users will create their own utility routines and thus create their own system to be handled within our framework. Our past experience with the SDS 940 was reasonably successful in this regard. Our hard core system does not include compilers, file directories, or facilities of this nature. All such facilities are utility programs that are nonprivileged.

I would like at this point to discuss some aspects of our work on the current system and to begin by briefly describing the hardware and some of the functions assigned to it. The system, as we see it this year (and our viewpoint seems to change every year), is very much memory-oriented. We have put a large share of our effort into understanding the problems of storage systems: access time, latency, and so forth (where latency is not an exclusive property of drums—even core storage has latency of sorts). We have decided that for a medium sized time-sharing system, it is expedient to have a high bandwidth core storage. We think in terms of a 50 to 60 million characters-per-second transfer rate into and out of core. This has turned out to be fairly economical, and we are happy with it. With respect to secondary storage, we discount disparaging remarks about drum latency and plan to make extensive use of drum storage. A transfer rate (obtained from two simultaneously transferring drums) of from 10 to 12 million characters per second and capacity of from 30 to 40 million characters is planned. The third level of storage will be a disk with a 500 million character capacity and a relatively high transfer rate. For the whole system to fly, the central storage must be either complex or fast; we chose the complex route. Although most of our main memory is one microsecond, it includes a small, fast portion which causes it to appear to most of the processors to be a 200 nanosecond memory.

The memory is surrounded by processors, only one of which can be considered as a central processing unit. With respect to the CPU, it has been pointed out that there is a need for new types of central processors. We feel that this is correct, but on the other hand, we have a very limited staff. So for this year we are ignoring the CPU problem and going along with existing CPU's except to make them a little faster.

The other processors serve to handle certain tasks that can be handled in hardware conveniently and economically, One such task is that of memory management, that is, handling transfers between main memory, drums, and disks, and also just within main memory. We plan that all of this scheduling will be done by one processor—a processor which does not have storage of its own, but like all the other processors, shares the use of main memory. There are always communication problems between processors, and we have found that the best way to alleviate those problems is through sharing of common memory among all processors. This procedure leaves only small problems of temporarily locking various tables so that the processors don't interfere with each other.

Besides the CPU and the processor for managing memory, there are several other processors, one of which takes on the task of scheduling the CPU. When we first started looking several years ago for hardware that was amenable to a time-sharing system, we paid a lot of attention to the facility for interrupts. We learned the hard way that classical interrupt systems are not the way to go; the scheduling problems are too numerous. We found ourselves with two scheduling policies: One was for the normal users in handling their tasks; the other, completely independent, for scheduling the interrupt routines. In a simple system this can work, but as the system grows in complexity, it becomes painful. Therefore, we eliminated interrupts from the CPU and assigned a processor to the sole task of scheduling the CPU.

Yet another function assigned to a separate processor is that of address mapping. We have provided the CPU with a conventional associative addresses translation mechanism that actually performs the address translation. The processor is used to interpret entries in several tables and load the translation mechanism appropriately.

Another function assigned to a separate processor is that of the character I/O. Its memory, as always, is main core so that its tables and buffer areas are accessible to other processors, particularly the CPU.

We have gone to hardware also to assist in the problem of reliability. We assign a second header to each record stored on the rotating devices. This header contains what we call a class code. For each transfer to or from the disk, for example, the transfer unit is instructed about this class code. A command to write on the disk includes a description of the class code; if it does not agree with the class code on the addressed record on the disk, writing is inhibited. This procedure doesn't eliminate the source of errors, but it insures catching them quickly. In the past we have experienced severe problems, such as reading a block of pointers and inadvertently getting a block of random data, which would then be used to systematically clobber numerous files. It's quite easy to make such mistakes. By comparing class codes, such errors are prevented.

Finally, a few words regarding the CPU. First, its general character is similar to that of the present CPU. Some additional instructions have been added, but otherwise the instructions and their format are very similar. Second, a restricted form of segmentation has been added that provides for 32 "segments" of 16K. Third, the protected entry facility of our current CPU has been extended to provide for restricted entry into a large collection of procedures. Finally, some of the protection features suggested by David C. Evans and Jean Yves LeClerc* have been included.

This latter facility provides for assigning accessibilities to directed lines between segments rather than to the segments themselves. Thus, for example,

*Evans and LeClerc, "Address Mapping and the Control of Access in an Interactive Computer," *Proceedings AFIPS Conf.*, XXX, SJCC 1967, 23–30.

we can provide a routine with a protected entry to an I/O routine that has in turn, access to a data buffer and a protected entry to an I/O driver routine; yet the initial routine has no direct access to either the buffer or the driver routine. It should be apparent that these facilities allow us to place a large number of the functions frequently associated with a resident, nonrestricted monitor into utility routines that have restricted capabilities and are therefore much more flexible in terms of modification, augmentation, or substitution by a user supplied routine.

What does all this leave for the monitor itself? Not very much; its current projected size is still under 4K. So much is done by the special processors and the utility programs that little is left for the monitor—and that conforms nicely to our initial goal.

Time-Sharing Software: What's Good and What's Bad

BRUCE W. ARDEN

Professor, Department of
Communication Sciences
University of Michigan

This conference is concerned with the problems associated with the computer handling of large data bases and the relation to time-sharing software is probably not immediately obvious. The relationship is of second order in that the processing of large quantities of data introduces a pressure for facility centralization, and a report on time-sharing software is a description of how one approach to centralization is proceeding.

The title implies some judgments, but no critique at the level of programming skill will be attempted. There is no reason to believe that the ratio of competent lines of code to incompetent lines of code in time-sharing is very different from that of other large, production software systems. Rather the observations that follow are general in nature and arise from some experience at the University of Michigan in the development of a large time-sharing package and a close association with the development of another.

The specific goal at Michigan has been the development of a general system in which a spectrum of operation is made available to the user. The range should extend from the highly interactive, terminal-oriented computation through remote job entry capability, and include conventional multi-programmed batch operation. The system was to be file oriented and contain many language processors. In retrospect it is probably more appropriate to call such a system a general multiprogrammed system rather than bias its application by the use of the adjective "time-sharing." It was also part of the original plan that, in accounting for the use of the system, the user would be charged only for that fraction of the facility actually employed. The conviction was of long standing at Michigan that such a system could be implemented only with a machine with a large virtual storage. An alternate description is to say that the machine must have hardware address translation from logical addresses to physical, with many more logical addresses than physical. Although there has been much debate on this issue, the conviction still remains that a system of the generality described cannot be produced without such a hardware facility. To be sure, a great deal can be accomplished with more conventional machines by restricting the capabilities at the interactive end of the spectrum or, alternately, dedicating the system to specialized interactive use.

MTS DEVELOPMENT

With these goals established, an IBM 360/67 was ordered and subsequently installed in January of 1967. It was a half duplex machine with 512K bytes of core storage. There was a somewhat naive hope that IBM's TSS system would meet the requirements posed by the middle of that year. It has turned out to be fortunate that the model 67 was preceded by a 360/50, which was used to support a model 7090 and some early work on the development of the graphical programs. To carry out the latter function, a simple, variable partition, multiprogrammed system was devised. The kernel of that early system was Lincoln Laboratories multiprogramming system (LLMPS). That system was simple, with a monitor which handled core-resident jobs in an RR fashion; these jobs could be started and terminated only from operators' consoles. In the face of the increasing development time of TSS, the decision was made to elaborate on this structure. A reentrant job to supervise terminal activity was written. This job was just one of the multiprogrammed group being handled by the revised monitor (now called UMMPS) and was called the Michigan Terminal System (MTS). It was necessary to write device support routines, line file routines for both private and public files, a command interpreter for file and device designation and manipulation, a dynamic loader, libraries of various sorts, and to modify existing language processors so that they could be included. Currently there are about eight language processors available under the MTS system. This programming work proceeded while running the model 67 as a multiprogrammed model 65 under MTS. The two level structure (that is, MTS running as a job in UMMPS) made it relatively easy to handle performance-critical routines at the higher level. Functions like reader and printer support and the statistical monitoring of the system were included as jobs that UMMPS would handle.

With the 512K machine run as a model 65 in a variable partition multiprogrammed manner, the number of terminals was effectively limited to six or fewer, because of storage constraints. The statistical monitoring showed about a 15 per cent processor load in this mode of operation. By November of 1967 MTS supervisor alterations and additions had been completed, and the change was made to run with the relocation of 24 bit addresses. This change affected only the supervisor. It required the addition of a paging drum processor routine, the establishment of page tables (accomplished by consulting chained page control blocks), and at the I/O interface, the transformation of virtual channel commands to real-address commands. The method of using the relocation hardware adopted is very simple. More sophisticated schemes are certainly possible. In essence the resident system was in segment 0, and the associated page tables produced the identity mapping. The user code is in segment 1 thus giving a total of 1,024K bytes of virtual storage. There is no inherent limitation, however, to a single segment; it is simply a matter of adding more page tables, and this has not yet been done. When the system started operating as a Model 67 the number of page-hours utilized increased dramatically as one would expect, and the processor utilization was monitored at about 60 per cent. This figure does not really represent a limit but is simply a reflection of the current load state. The expansion to the current maximum of 31 lines was made immediately.

There is an anecdote worth mentioning at this point. Shortly after the relocation system became operative, a user appeared with a complaint. His Fortran program, he said, had been operating satisfactorily for some days until he increased the size of his principal array slightly, so that it was now 90 by 1200 double words. A little arithmetic shows that this huge array plus the rest of his program exceeds the 1024K byte current limit. The encouraging thing was that he had been operating multiprogrammed, through batch, at close to that maximum of virtual storage without difficulty and had been getting productive work done.

Currently two or three batch streams are run in a fairly elementary way. They are simply multiprogrammed from assigned reader-printer pairs. A batch monitor is currently under development that will simplify the operator's task and improve the loading on printers but probably not markedly increase the throughput. The paging mechanism is about the simplest that could be devised. It is pure demand paging in which pages are put on a page-out queue but not written out until necessary. Moreover, the queue is reordered by observing the storage reference bits. Any pages that have been referenced are continually put at the bottom of the page-out queue. To be sure, one can construct poor performance examples with this kind of operation, but the important fact is that, in observing a realistic mix of problems, the algorithm does not seem to give any significant difficulty. A multiple queue slot sorting technique is used for the paging drum. Read commands are given preference over write commands, and channel programs are constructed which keep the paging drum transmission as continuous as the load allows. The current bottleneck seems to arise from the file orientation of the system and the competition for disk accesses, rather than its paging structure. There are some advantages and disadvantages to a system of this sort.

Advantages:

1. The two level control structure (i.e., the multiprogrammed system and the terminal supervisor) make the addition of high priority programs straightforward and make the checkout of the second level system much simpler.

2. The incremental structure is a great virtue. The ability to augment an ongoing system, which is continually being tested at its present level of development, is much superior to the grand design implemented all at once.

3. With the relocation control software localized, there is no inherent reason why user programs could not run in different address relocation modes. In the 360 case there are 24 bit address and 32 bit address relocation options.

Disadvantages:

1. Currently there are no shared files. That is, they are either private or public and not limited public or shared. However, this feature is being added.

2. With the exception of the reentrant resident routines there is no provision for common code. The inclusion of this capability would be a major addition to MTS.

3. The system error recovery capability of MTS is very limited. Again this is not an inherent design limitation, but it would involve a large system change in order to implement. Specifically, the now-fixed subdivision between resident and nonresident code would have to be made much more flexible.

TSS REVIEW

To use the vernacular, the University of Michigan Computing Center has, in large measure, "kept the faith" in the organization and goals (but not in the time schedule) of TSS. The current state of this ambitious system is probably pretty well known. It would not be instructive to recite the contents of recent IBM blue letters. There have been two modifications of this system since the October release. The glaring deficiencies of the system are being fixed. Specifically, the command language is being rewritten, the table driven scheduler is under implementation, and a revised bulk I/O processor (which will produce a reasonable batch monitor) is under development. Moreover, the continual debugging has increased the stability to a respectable level and execution; a duplex system is under implementation. The comparison given below is largely with respect to MTS, but some of the observations have a broader relevance.

Advantages:

1. The system is designed to handle programs written in shared code form. The language processors are written this way and the code produced by these processors is in this form.

2. Access methods are much more elaborate than simply line files, which are, in essence, a specialized index sequential form.

3. The system error recovery capability is very good.

4. The internal structure is reasonably clean; it could be reworked.

5. The performance of the assembler and Fortran compiler are good, compared to their analogs in the standard system.

Disadvantages:

1. There is a higher core threshold for MTS equivalent performance, under light load. There is a conjecture, not yet settled, that at some point, under heavy load, the system size distinction vanishes. The statement is based on the argument that the common code begins to pay off and that, even if the fixed overhead is greater, for a large number of users the fraction of overhead per user diminishes.

2. Initial virtual memory cannot be released. The current strategy is to have a large initial virtual memory. This does, however, tie up auxiliary storage which decreases system performance.

3. Mixed relocation strategies cannot readily be handled at the same time.

SYSTEM ACCOUNTING

One of the educational experiences of these developments is that the charge-for-what-is-used philosophy forces the system to be general in the sense that it must offer the spectrum of types of operations referred to earlier. The accounting scheme described below is currently being used in MTS, which is the principal operation system at the University at this time. A very similar recording function is being installed in TSS. The initial reaction may be one of horror to the apparent complexity of this system. However, after some experience, it is now believed to be one of the strong points, rather than detriments, of these complex systems, because it introduces to the user the capability of making some realistic cost estimates in an area that has been traditionally a fuzzy one in computing. Besides that, the measurements needed are rather natural by-products of the kinds of systems being described and, somewhat surprisingly, do not constitute a heavy overhead. The variables and rates and costs are employed as shown below.

T_t = Terminal connect time (hours)

T_p = Processor time (hours)

T_f = Time that file storage is used since the last run and during current run (hours)

$M_v(t)$ = Pages of virtual memory used (changes dynamically with time)

$S_f(t)$ = Pages of file storage used (changes dynamically during a run— fixed between runs)

N_r = Number of cards read

N_c = Number of cards punched

N_p = Number of lines printed (not terminal)

C_b = Cost of batch run

C_t = Cost of terminal run

Terminal Cost	Tenancy	Processor	File	Bulk I/O

$$C_t = \alpha \int dT_t \; + \beta \int M_v(t)\,|dT_t \; + \gamma \int dT_p \; + \delta \int S_f(t)\,dT_f$$

$$C_b = \qquad\quad + \beta \int M_v(t)\,dT_p \; + \gamma \int dT_p \; + \delta \int S_f(t)\,dT_f + aN_r + bN_c + cN_p$$

Rates			
	α dollars/hour	a = dollars/1000 cards	
	β dollars/page	b = dollars/1000 cards	
	γ dollars/hour	c = dollars/1000 lines	
	δ dollars/page hour		

The current practice is to allocate computing dollars as any other regular budget item. It is then up to the manager or head of the local unit to determine the strategy for using these dollars. He can choose from the extremes of minimum elapsed time to computing project completion, to maximum processor page hours, per dollar expended.

SUMMARY

The desirable, or good, developments that have appeared in the time-sharing or general software development are:

1. A realistic accounting that allows the user to choose his own strategy among the spectrum of operational modes these systems allow.

2. The incremental development of software is much preferable to the all-at-once general system.

3. The basic file orientation solves many problems in a general computing environment. More specifically, a capability for shared files lets user sub-

groups operate on private developments without the central operating group having to assume responsibility for these quasi-public files.

4. Sophisticated system error recovery is vital for general systems of any size. That is, retry and diagnostic procedures sufficient to recover from spurious machine errors are simply a necessity when a large number of users are on line.

5. Problems exceeding the simple physical capacity of the machine can be effectively handled in a virtual memory machine. Programs to monitor software and hardware performance have been developed and are a vital part of debugging and system improvement.

In retrospect, there have been some undesirable aspects or more blatantly bad results.

1. The interactive or conversational capability has been emphasized to the exclusion of the other end of the operational spectrum. Specifically, it has been found in the two observed cases that a good batch capability has had to be retrofitted into an already existing software design. This is particularly forced on one if realistic accounting is to be implemented as described.

2. It seems necessary to relearn an old lesson. A very general system is ideal only if you have a very general environment. Or stated another way, a special purpose system is superior if it meets the needs.

3. The relationship between the apparent efficiency of initial binding of program modules, and the later inefficiencies of being unable to release prebound modules has led, overwhelmingly, to the initial binding philosophy.

4. When we consider the 360 implementations, the existence of two address relocations schemes has added considerable complication.

Finally, in the balance, there is much to be encouraged about. Real progress has been and is being made in the development of such ambitious systems. It seems very unlikely that all of these efforts will lead to an evolutionary dead end.

Data Management on Wall Street

FRANK M. VERZUH

Management Consultant
Boston, Massachusetts

Since the title of this article covers a lot of territory, I shall delimit the scope by eliminating certain areas. The back office operations of member firms are identical in function; however, the method of implementation varies among firms. The small firms cannot afford to rent or purchase EDP equipment of their own. Hence, their work is done on a service bureau basis. The Midwest Stock Exchange recognized the plight of the small firm and provided a centralized bookkeeping operation for those member firms who wish to avail themselves of this service. The Midwest Centralized Bookkeeping Service has proved to be highly successful.

In 1965 the New York Stock Exchange established a Central Computer Accounting Corporation to provide computerized brokerage accounting service for its member firms. However, the implementation of the CCAC program ran into difficulty and the project was abandoned in 1967.

This paper will not consider the details of the accounting services involved with the calculation of purchase and sale data, printing of confirmations and statements, margin accounts, and bookkeeping for securities traded on the exchanges and over the counter. I omit the back office operations in this presentation because there is too much other material to cover.

The following topics will be considered:

1. An overall view of the EDP operations at the NYSE,
2. A description of the Market Data Syatem at NYSE,
3. A discussion of the high speed ticker service,
4. A description of the Voice Answer Back (VAB) quotation service,
5. A description of the Bunker-Ramo, Scantlin, and Ultronics market services,

6. A description of Merrill Lynch Security Opinion Request service,
7. A description of the Central Certificate Service program,
8. A description of the Time Series Decomposition Analysis (TSDA) program,
9. A study of share volume using the TSDA program,
10. A study of mathematical models.

Succeeding sections describe each of the above-mentioned topics.

1. OVERALL VIEW OF THE EDP OPERATIONS AT THE NYSE

The Electronic Systems Center at the New York Stock Exchange is one of the largest computer service centers in existence. In addition to the multiple System 360 computer installations, there are a number of sophisticated data handling devices on the floor of the exchange.

900 MOVING TICKER DISPLAY

The Exchange's "900" moving ticker display is 45 feet long by 3 feet high and displays letters and numerals through a combination of pneumatics and electronics. It is the largest existing device for displaying continuous

Fig. 1 The 900 moving ticker display in operation at the NYSE

stock ticker information. It shows stock symbols and last-sale prices within the same second that they are sent over the ticker network. The key to the display is an electronically activated jet-air device that forms traveling letters and numerals—composed from 23,000 luminescent colored disks. The seven-inch high luminous yellow-green characters displayed against a black background can be read at distances up to 300 feet. The "900" moving ticker display consists of a track around which travel 180 rectangular panels 5 inches wide and 23 inches high. Within each panel there are 115 plastic disks, 7/8 of an inch in diameter, painted black on one side and yellow-green on the other. Mounted on pivot rods, the disks are flipped by air jets to compose the characters needed for recording transactions—letters for stock symbols, digits for whole numbers and fractions as needed. The photograph in Fig. 1 shows the "900" moving ticker in operation on the floor of the Exchange.

CARD READERS

In 1966 a specially designed, optically scanned card reader was installed at each trading post on the floor of the Exchange. Reporters fill out an IBM card with the last sale or the bid-ask price as required. Actually, the IBM card is so designed that as many as three trades and one bid-ask price may be reported on a single card. The card is optically scanned, and the information is automatically inserted into the Market Data System computer. Previously the Reporter prepared slips which were manually key punched before the information was sent to the ticker tape.

Figure 2 illustrates the form and content of a typical optical scan card. The sample card is for Post 17; other cards identical in format are used at other posts and have appropriate stock symbols.

ODD LOT ORDER SWITCHING

Since the processing of odd-lot orders is much simpler than round-lot orders, a standardized teletypewriter order format was created in 1965, and the odd-lot orders were separated and diverted to a location beneath the trading floor. Preliminary tests indicate that a computer can execute the odd-lot order if it has the related last-sale information. The two odd-lot firms have computer programs well developed and undergoing test. It is necessary to coordinate the computer with the odd-lot associate broker on the floor of the Exchange who is executing the round-lot offsetting transactions.

A limited test of the automation of the odd-lot operation was made in 1966 when the odd-lot orders for stocks traded at Post 17 were switched to the basement. The data on these orders related to last-sale information was

NYSE
MARKET DATA SYSTEMS COMPUTER

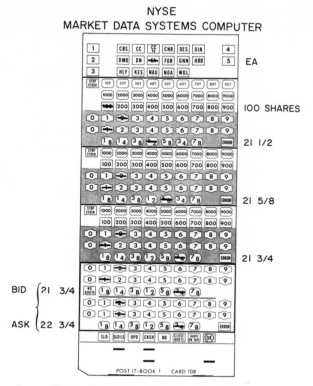

Fig. 2   Reporters last-sale optical scan card

provided by the Market Data System. These tests have proved successful, and plans are underway for complete computer handling of orders for both mechanized and nonmechanized commission firms.

2. MARKET DATA SYSTEM AT NYSE

The Market Data System at the NYSE contains duplexed IBM 7010 computers. Time sharing is used to provide both ticker and quotation services simultaneously using one computing system. The duplexed computer may be switched on line (manually) in about 30 seconds. As a matter of fact, the same system is also used for on-the-job training of floor operations personnel in the new method of reporting trade and quote data. Hence, three operations proceed concurrently, each independent of the other, although the computer equipment and files are shared. Thus we have an impressive demonstration of time sharing at NYSE.

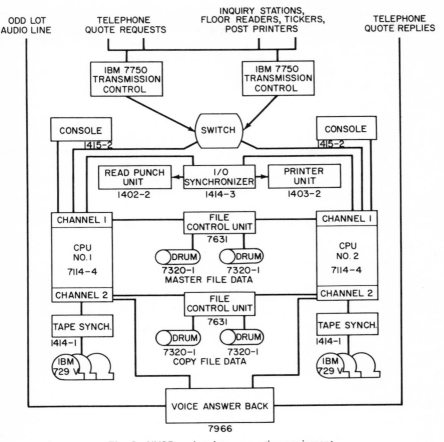

Fig. 3   NYSE market data computing equipment

Admittedly, the installation employs "second generation" computer equipment for the Market Data System. This is so because the system was initially conceived in 1959 and implemented during the early part of 1964—before the "third generation" computers were announced. Nevertheless, the Market Data System is designed to handle trading volume of up to 16 million shares a day. Eventually the system will be converted to third generation equipment. Figure 3 illustrates the principal elements of the Market Data System.

3. THE HIGH SPEED TICKER SYSTEM

During the early sixties it became apparent that the old "black box" 500 Ticker would not be able to handle the high volumn on the NYSE. Development was initiated, and the 900 "high speed" Ticker was installed in 1964. The 900 Ticker handled the high volume in 1965 with brief periods of lateness on only 33 days. A maximum delay of 13 minutes occurred on December 6th when the reported volume reached 11.4 million shares.

Since there are higher volumes coming, several short cuts have been approved by the Board of Governors. To conserve the number of characters transmitted during heavy activity, consecutive same-price sales are "bunched" at such times. Appropriate ticker notices precede and follow the use of this procedure. It must be recognized that there is a top speed at which the ticker may operate—otherwise the rate may be too high for comprehension by the viewing public.

Generally speaking, the 900 Ticker performs satisfactorily even during the present-day high volumes, since the deletion of leading digits further minimizes the number of transmitted digits during heavy volume. However, when the volume exceeds 12 million shares, the tape does run late.

4. THE VOICE ANSWER BACK QUOTATION SERVICE

The new voice-answer-back quotation service provides a spoken message containing last sale and up-to-the-market bid-asked quotations. In addition the open, high, low, last sale, and volume for any listed stock is available. The spoken message is generated from a selection of prerecorded words and numbers recorded on a magnetic drum.

The system is designed to handle 150 incoming and 150 outgoing calls simultaneously—with a total daily capacity of 400,000 calls. There is a capacity for 1000 telephone subscribers to use the service. By dialing a four-digit number, a subscriber can receive up-to-the market bid and asked and last-sale information. Since this is a telephone inquiry service, for economic reasons the service is generally restricted to the Manhattan area.

Figure 4 illustrates the relationship between the 1000 telephone subscribers, the 19 floor readers, the post printers, the voice-answer-back equipment and the high speed ticker system.

5. BUNKER-RAMO, SCANTLIN, AND ULTRONIC SERVICES

The high speed ticker at the NYSE is the source of the stock data supplied to Bunker-Ramo, Scantlin, and Ultronics. Each of the three services has a desk top interrogation unit brokers use to get instant information.

Bunker-Ramo has 11,000 Telequote III desk-top interrogators installed in 1500 brokerage offices. Telequote III has a small cathode ray tube which displays up-to-the-minute information from all major stock exchanges and the

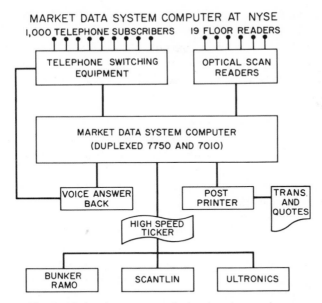

MARKET DATA SYSTEM COMPUTER AT NYSE

Fig. 4 Market data system and related services equipment

over the counter market. By pushing the appropriate buttons, the broker may obtain the latest price, volume, high, low, bid-ask, and much other data on any stock. The CRT display is of the right dimension to appeal to the user.

The ticker information from the several exchanges is fed to the Tele-Center—an extensive on-line financial data processing center located at 75 Varick Street in New York City. The TeleCenter distributes the stock data to the Telequote III units over a high speed network of communication lines and satellite computers located in key cities. Bunker-Ramo also offers Tele-quote Trends which displays a series of stock averages and trends in vertical format. It also markets a new horizontal ticker display with traveling characters called Teletrade.

Scantlin developed the first desk-top interrogation unit—Quotron—in 1961. The original unit provided stock data in the form of a printed tape. Although the printed tape was quite popular with the investor, it is rather expensive for the broker, who is interested in only the last price or the bid and asked. In order to keep the Quotron price competitive, a visual display unit was later added. Recently, Scantlin has combined forces with Dow Jones and the two have produced Dow Vue—a video screen carrying New York and Amex last sale prices.

Ultronics produced its Stockmaster desk interrogation unit in 1962. Stockmaster displays its stock data on Nixie tubes. It also provides averages, indexes, and market volumes. At present there are some 10,000 Stockmaster interrogation units and 3000 Lectroscan display units installed. The Stockmaster was the first interrogation unit with "simultaneous access"—any number of brokers in a given office can use the system at one time.

These three market services provide the broker with finger-tip control of the latest market condition of any stock. Certainly the burden on the broker has been minimized by the availability of these market services. As a matter of fact, the availability of these services provides the public investor with a medium for keeping track of a particular stock. As a result, mergers and acquisitions may be effected without the prior knowledge of the security analyst. Previously the customer's security analyst was well aware of any contemplated acquisition long before it became a fact. Today, the desk-top interrogation unit provides the investor with pertinent stock market information without tipping his hand to the security analyst. As a result, impending acquistions or mergers are announced as complete surprises to the investment community.

In my opinion these market services will reduce the technical requirements of the stock broker. Since the interrogation unit provides fingertip access to most financial data on stocks, the stock broker does not have to be as knowledgeable—the computer remembers the data for him. Hence, we may see less technically qualified personnel acting as stock brokers.

6. MERRILL LYNCH SECURITY OPINION REQUEST SERVICE

One of the principal functions of the security analyst is to provide research opinions on the stocks which he covers. At Merrill, Lynch, Pierce, Fenner & Smith these research opinions have been placed on a computer so that any one of the 3500 stocks may be queried using the security opinion request service. The research opinions are stored on the magnetic disks on a computer located in New York City. The private line network connecting the 170 branch offices to the computer is used to transmit the security opinions to the inquiring customer.

The private line network is shared by orders and security opinions. Naturally the orders are given priority and there may be considerable delay in receipt of the security opinions when the order volume is high. A customer at any branch office may call in and request a QRQ on any of the 3500 stocks. The request is teletyped to New York by the branch office. The local account representative then telephones the customer and gives him the message. The response time may be 1 or 2 minutes when the volume is light.

Figure 5 illustrates the interconnection of equipment used in the quotation request service. If desired, anyone located near one of the 170 branch offices

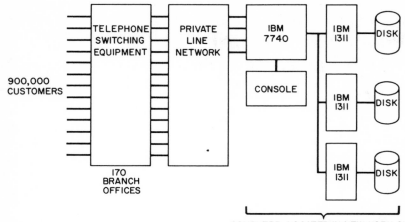

COMPUTER LOCATED IN NEW YORK CITY

RESEARCH OPINIONS MAY BE OBTAINED FOR ANY ONE OF 3,500 STOCKS IN
I OR 2 MINUTES

NOTE: Private Line Network is shared by orders and quotations. During heavy volume there may be a delay in
quotations because orders have priority.

Fig. 5 Stock market quotation request service

may telephone his account representative and request a security quotation. The response time is governed by the volume of traffic on the private line network. In effect each of the 900,000 customers has access to this service.

Figure 6 illustrates the content of an actual quotation request. It should be observed that a sort of jargonese is used to record the security opinion. Abbreviations and misspellings are present and are quite acceptable, since the reader understands the language used. The shorthand script reduces the number of characters required and thereby increases the maximum size of the total message.

7. CENTRAL CERTIFICATE SERVICE

At the present time transactions in listed securities that take place on the floor of the New York Stock Exchange are cleared or settled through the Stock Clearing Corporation (SCC) and delivery or payment for the securities involved is made through that corporation. Since the process of offsetting purchases and sales of the same security on a given day by the same Clearing Member (CM) requires delivery of only the *net* balance resulting from this process, SCC is able to eliminate the physical delivery of some 30 per cent of the total number of shares cleared or settled through it.

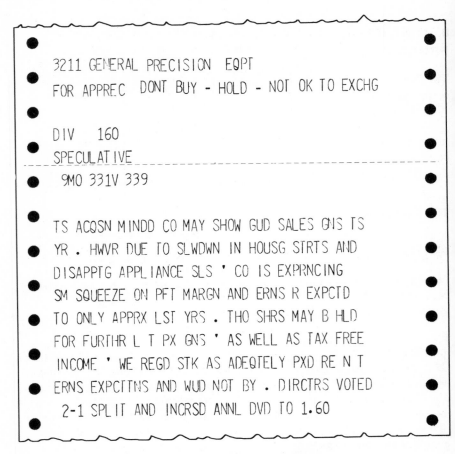

Fig. 6 Typical example of a quotation request

The Central Certificate Service was designed to further decrease the physical movement of shares. The system operates like a checking account. Clearing members will place their stock certificates on deposit with the CCS. To effect the delivery of shares to another Clearing Member, the firm would instruct CCS to decrease the number of shares in its account and to increase the number of shares of the receiving firm. The transfer would be made by computer but no physical transfer of certificates would occur. As a result, the system is expected to eliminate 75 per cent of the physical handling of securities.

Once CCS becomes fully operational, there should be a considerable reduction in back office operations, and the current backlog on high volume days should be reduced considerably.

8. TIME SERIES DECOMPOSITION AND ANALYSIS PROGRAM

The Time Series Analysis program decomposes a given time series into four components:

1. *Cyclic* (C) fluctuation—a slow, cyclical change that is recurrent; however, the duration of the cycle changes slowly under different business conditions.

2. *Trend* (T) variation which exhibits the long-term character of the series.

3. *Seasonal* (S) fluctuation recurring at particular times in the base period. The seasonal component is periodic (as a rule) and may be predicted.

4. *Irregular* (I) fluctuations which are random in character and impossible to predict in advance.

In addition to these components, various combinations of components are computed. The cyclic-trend (CT) component is very useful in the prediction of future values of the function.

The TSDA program was used to analyze the NYSE Share Volume. Figure 7 illustrates the form of the cyclic-trend components of the average daily share volume. Examination of the cyclic-trend component reveals an average daily share volume of 5 million shares in 1964. Three years later (1967) the volume had doubled to over 10 million shares. The rapid rate of rise made accurate forecasting of share volume rather difficult.

9. STUDY OF SHARE VOLUMES USING THE TSDA PROGRAM

Intelligent planning of the size of the office staff at a brokerage firm or an Exchange is influenced by the forecast of the expected share volume. Various methods have been used to forecast the share volume. Since some of the forecasts have been too low, there are many brokerage firms with understaffed back offices. Naturally this contributes to the delay in processing of back office operations on high-volume days.

The TSDA program may be used to help forecast the share volume at the different exchanges. TSDA studies have been made of the share volume at the New York Stock Exchange, the American Stock Exchange, the Midwest Exchange, the Boston Exchange, and the Philadelphia Exchange. Examination of the cyclic-trend component and application of crude extrapolation formulae to the cyclic-trend component provide an indication of the

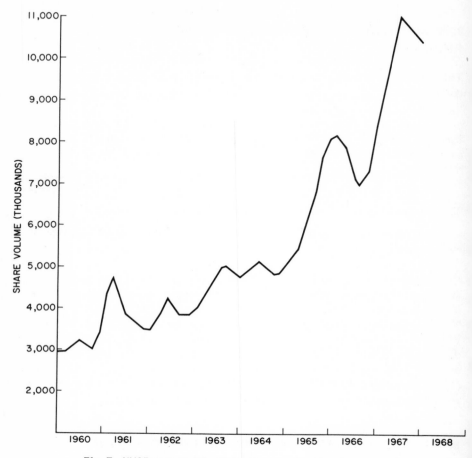

Fig. 7   NYSE average daily share volume, cyclical trend component

magnitude of the projected share volume. Such techniques have been used with success at Merrill Lynch since 1961.

It is clear that one of the most important problems facing the financial community is the hiring and training of an adequate back office force. The current lack of adequate staff is responsible for the backlog in the processing of back office operations.

10. STUDY OF MATHEMATICAL MODELS

The success in developing a mathematical model of the stock market is strongly influenced by a knowledge of the related variables. There are a large number of independent variables that affect the behavior of the stock market. The following items must be considered:

1. Select a limited set of variables which will be used as input to the regression model,

2. Determine the appropriate time period and the particular time intervals at which observations are made,

3. Determine the component of the input variable which is to be used,

4. Determine the need for a time *lead* or time *lag* among the different variables,

5. Determine the particular independent variables to be used in the STKVOL or STKPRC regression equations.

By the application of the TSDA program to the likely candidate variables, a selected set may be chosen, and answers to the above-mentioned criteria may be obtained.

There are many areas in which regression equations may be effectively applied. Mathematical models of the following types have been studied:

1. Agriculture—factors affecting the supply and prices of hogs,

2. Automobile industry—factors affecting the demand for and sale of automobiles,

3. Building industry—factors affecting the number of new housing starts,

4. Business models—factors affecting the rate of industrial production,

5. Retail sales models—factors affecting the sales of consumer goods,

6. Stock market models—factors affecting the share volume of the New York Stock Exchange.

It must be stressed that certain industries are subject to change. In such cases certain of the independent variables must be replaced by new, more dominant variables as the need arises.

The preceding sections describe some of the data management activities present on Wall Street. The lack of an adequate number of trained personnel in the back offices of brokerage firms is responsible for the delay in delivery of certificates.

Peripheral Equipment for Data Management

TEAGUE N. LEIBOFF

Research Engineer, Nortronics
A Division of Northrop Corporation
Palos Verdes, California

For the Adams Associates' *Computer Characteristics Quarterly*, they advertise: "A new section lists the salient features of more than 800 peripheral devices. . . ." These 800 devices fall under the categories of auxiliary storage, magnetic tape units, punched card equipment, line printers, perforated tape equipment, and display terminals. As large as this number seems, it actually includes only part of the peripheral equipment types presently available to the data management system designer.

Computers have progressed from units having less than 1,000 words of memory and 200-microsecond access times (in those cave-man days of the early 1950's) to our present "third-generation" computers having 100,000-word main memories and one-half microsecond access times. Features such as general purpose registers, asynchronous I/O busses, read-only memories, and nanosecond scratch pads have demonstrated great advances in mainframe technology. During this same period, however, peripheral devices have had a much slower growth rate. Those early 1950 computers used magnetic tape for secondary storage and had line printers and card readers quite similar to those used in today's systems. Today's peripherals are faster and more sophisticated and, in many cases, less costly, but they are still basically the same as before. Perhaps the most dramatic advances in peripheral devices can be found in the random (sequential) access auxiliary storage units and in the alphanumeric and graphic cathode-ray tube display terminals.

Selecting the peripherals for your particuar data management system can be a very complicated and time consuming task—the selection of peripheral types is broad and the nuances of difference within each category makes selection seem an almost arbitrary thing. Trade-offs have to be made, and all sides of the problem analyzed to get the proper weighting of features and capabilities as expressed by both the systems analyst and the design engineer.

To simplify this discussion of peripheral equipment, I have divided it into only two classes: auxiliary storage devices and I/O devices. I include only those equipments under direct computer control.

AUXILIARY STORAGE

For the storage of large masses of data directly accessible to the computer, magnetic tape units are used in almost all present data handling systems. The recording medium consists of a cellulose acetate or Mylar (polyester) tape with finely divided iron-oxide particles embedded in vinyl resin. Rolls of magnetic tape are available in lengths up to 5,000 feet and at common widths of 1/2 to 1 inch. Small electro-magnets, or heads, are used to record, read, and erase data. Heads are grouped together so that from 7 to 15 tracks can be recorded side-by-side on $\frac{1}{2}$-inch tape.

The tape transport, or handler, is the equipment used to hold the tape on spools and move it past the head. Since the transport is required to accelerate the tape rapidly during stop and start operations, reel units are designed to maintain slack between the drive assembly and reels. Motor speeds are controlled by sensing techniques, such as follower arms, pneumatic control, photoelectric sensing, and weight measurement. Transports with pneumatic control are usually larger and heavier but have capability for higher speed and shorter start-stop times.

Current technology permits tapes with a maximum storage density of 1,600 bits per inch, although 200, 556, and 800 bits per inch are in greater usage. The tape is moved at rates of up to 150 inches per second. Most tape units will read data forwards or backwards. In most units data is recorded in the 7-bit IBM or 9-bit ASCII codes.

Spools of tape can easily be loaded or removed so that large quantities of data, programs, and records can be stored, off-line, to be replaced and used when required. Programs and data bases can thus be transferred from one computing center to another, making the magnetic tape unit an important I/O device as well as an auxiliary memory. Magnetic tape is the least expensive medium of auxiliary storage, and magnetic tape units outnumber all other auxiliary storage devices presently in use. But the length of time required to serially access a specific record (up to several minutes) has diminished its importance in modern data processing.

RANDOM ACCESS STORAGE

As data management becomes more and more responsive to the needs of the user and the capabilities of the computer, a real-time, direct-access philosophy of data processing is developing. The entire data base is connected to the processor at all times; any data may be retrieved on request in fractions of a second. The techniques of random or sequential access storage makes this feasible. The devices currently used are magnetic drums, disk files, magnetic card systems, and tape loop units.

The fastest (and most expensive!) of the random access devices is the head-per-track drums and disks. These units rotate at speeds up to 3,600 revolutions per minute (sometimes up to 10,000 revolutions per minute for small drums) and have a read and write head for each track. Storage density is as much as 2,000 bits per inch. Data is often transferred at a megacycle rate, but the access or latency time is considered to be the time it takes for one-half revolution and ranges between 2.5 and 35 milliseconds. By stacking large diameter disks and then writing on both surfaces of each disk, as many as 5,000 heads (tracks) have been assembled on 12 surfaces for a 400-million bit head-per-track storage system.

The cost per bit can be significantly lowered and the drum or disk file increased in size by using a single read-write head per surface. The access time goes up, since the head must be positioned over the selected track. This increases the latency time from an average of 50 to as much as 200 milliseconds. Several storage devices use multiple heads mounted on the moving arm. This compromise permits increased track density and faster arm movement. The largest drums store up to 7 billion bits, and the largest disk files as much as 15 billion (approximately equal to 75 $10\frac{1}{2}$-inch spools of densely packed magnetic tape).

Several of the new disk units have replaceable disks, permitting data and programs to be removed and stored, transferred, and replaced as simply as with magnetic tapes.

Another direct access auxiliary storage device is the magnetic card unit. It consists of a drive assembly that moves a tray or cartridge of magnetically coated plastic cards to a mechanism that removes one card at a time and wraps it around a rotating drum. The read-write heads are then positioned over a track on this card. Because of the several mechanical motions involved, the latency time can be as high as one second when a new track on a new card from a different cartridge is accessed. Storage of as many as 4 billion bits is available, and the cost per bit is considerably less than the cost per bit for drums and disks.

A tape-loop memory utilizing eight 30-inch continuous magnetic tapes with an average access time of about 100 milliseconds is also available. This is one of the least expensive systems, providing approximately 50 million bits of storage for under $20,000.

Taking a peek at the future, one sees vastly improved thin-film memories, optical-laser memories, and thermoplastic memory systems. These will ultimately be mass produced, using large-scale integrated circuits, so that costs will be competitive with the current electromechanical devices. These new memories would be a directly addressable extension of the computer's memory

and would have enough capacity for the larger, more inclusive, data bases
and programs of the future.

I/O DEVICES

I/O peripheral equipment is a term generally applied to those components
of a computing system used for transfer of data to and from the computer
and for manipulation of data outside the computer itself. They may be as
simple as the DEC interrupt keyboard shown in Fig. 1 or as complex as the
Anti-Submarine Warfare tactical training console built by Lockheed for the
U.S. Naval Training Device Center in San Diego (Fig. 2). In any application,
the one necessary requirement for an I/O device is modification of data, so
that it can be accepted by the computer during input or presented in a usable
form to the operator during output

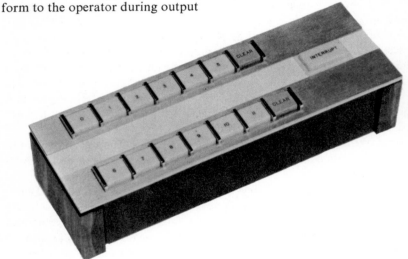

Fig. 1   Console pushbuttons—DEC 338 programmed buffered display

Today, despite the large increase of on-line programming, the large major-
ity of programs, files, and data are key-punched on cards prior to initial
loading in the computer. The 80-column Hollerith card is prevalent, and
today's computing facilities utilize more space for card storage than for the
computing hardware. These cards are punched, sorted, collated, and dupli-
cated in machinery independent of the computer. The card reader and a com-
puter-driven card punch are on-line to the computer. The readers handle a
maximum of 1,400 cards per minute. (Almost 2,000 characters per second.)
Off-line card-to-magnetic-tape converters are gaining widespread acceptance,

Fig. 2 Command and Control Center—U. S. Navy's antisubmarine warfare training center in San Diego, California, containing Northrop-Nortronics Vigicon display system

so expensive computing time need not be wasted by the comparatively slow process of card handling.

A first cousin to the punched card is the perforated paper tape. Although data on paper tape cannot be sorted, edited, and items deleted or added, paper tape is much simpler to handle and permits computer entry at equal speeds. Speed ranges from 25 characters per second in the slowest of mechanical readers to a maximum of 2,000 characters per second in the fastest optical readers. Perforated paper tape units perform many off-line operations such as transmitting and receiving computer-teletypewriter communications and controlling digital plotters.

Information retrieved from an automated data system must be output to the user in a meaningful and usable form. Sometimes a simple indicator lamp giving a yes or no answer is adequate, but for the most part some form of written document is required. For simple responses to queries, numerical solutions to problems, or short specific items of retrieved data, a typewriter output terminal is the simplest and most cost effective device. In the "new world of time-sharing," the teletypewriter console outnumbers all others as a remote terminal. Here the typewriter keyboard is also the input device, and much programming talent is expended in making the man-typewriter dialogue responsive to the man.

OUTPUT PRINTERS

For high speed printing of large quantities of data, a line printer—the large electromechanical device that often dominates the computer room—is required. Printing 100 to 160 characters per line at up to 1, 250 lines per minute

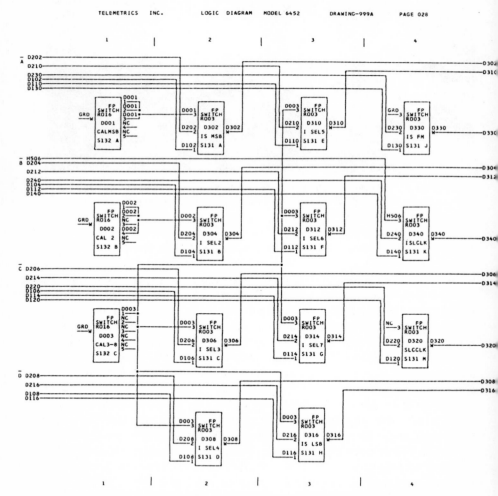

Fig. 3 Computer drawn schematic, using an IBM 1132 line printer

on multiple copies, it turns out huge quantities of paper. Several nonimpact type printers have been developed. An electrostatic printer capable of outputting 30,000 lines per minute, with its paper moving at nearly 100 inches per second, was built by Radiation, Inc. However, the cost of this system is so high it is prohibitive for most applications. There are several thermal printers available. CRT-photo printers are also on the market, but these require special paper, and for the most part, their output quality is not equal to that of the mechanical impact printers.

High speed printing of data frequently overloads the ability of the user. What computer user has not been innundated with paper? And in its tabulated, rigidly structured format information is often hard to use, difficult to understand, and usually impossible to digest. Remember the old adage about a picture being worth a thousand words—Why not present information pictorially or graphically? Plotting one variable against another has been a common method of providing usable data in engineering, science, and business. Figure 3 is an example of some of the ingenious programming performed to present pictorial information using a standard line printer.

Digital plotters have been designed for graphic recording. The incremental digital plotter, with accuracies of up to 0.0025 inches and plotting speed of $4\frac{1}{2}$ inches per second at costs of under $7,000 for on-line applications, makes this device an attractive peripheral for even small data systems. CRT plotting devices, using vector and line drawing techniques where an image is plotted on the face of the CRT and then photographed on 16- or 35-millimeter film, are faster (and, naturally, more expensive) than the incremental plotters. A high speed processor and photographic enlarger can present hard copy within a few minutes at rates up to two finished $8\frac{1}{2}$- by 11-inch pages per second. These devices are an order-of-magnitude more expensive than the digital incremental or analog plotters, and plotting accuracies are lower. Greater use of digital plotters will be made in the business computer field for outputting sales charts, stock analysis, trend forecasting, and other graphs, in the near future.

CRT DISPLAY TERMINALS

During the past few years no set of peripheral devices has come of age as quickly as the CRT display terminal. During the 1967 Fall Joint Computer Conference, there were as many as two dozen different CRT alphanumeric display terminals on hand (and working), and about half that number of graphical displays. Most of these displays use a 14- to 24-inch diagonal cathode-ray tube. Many are complete man-machine consoles containing a keyboard and computer function monitor. The display console permits the user direct access to the computer and the data base under computer control.

The input request and the output response can be presented in plain language. Display programs listing glossaries and formats can assist the user in retrieving information and can simplify the methods of inserting data into the system.

Most alphanumeric displays have their own refresh memory so that formatting, entering of keyboard information, editing, and making corrections can be performed without using valuable computing time. The total information is transferred between the display and the computer in rapid bursts. Some of these consoles contain light-pens, joy-stick cursor controls, and hardcopier attachments. The cost of the terminals is still fairly high (when compared with the teletypewriter), but new display units using memory display tubes or commercial T.V. receivers may bring the costs into a competitive position. The graphic display, subject of a previous symposium, offers an added dimension to man-machine communications.

DIRECT I/O TECHNIQUES

To simplify entry of large quantities of data, many devices are now in use for the direct reading of printed copy. From the magnetic-ink check-readers and devices requiring special character fonts for recognition, a family of optical readers has become available which scans whole printed or typewritten pages at rates of up to 2,400 characters per second. Much research in the recognition of handwriting is presently in progress. An IBM system, using restricted hand-printed characters, obtains recognition accuracies on the order of 95 per cent. This shows promise but falls far short of acceptable commercial performance. An interesting input device for use with a graphic display is the RAND tablet. This is an electronic scratch pad which translates the motion of an electronic pencil to computer coordinates, retracing the drawn lines on the face of the CRT.

As we make our computers more and more responsive to man, we approach the time when we can communicate with them using common speech. This becomes increasingly attractive as we establish additional computer terminals using standard telephone lines and circuits. Because of the complex wave-forms generated and because of the differences in pitch, delivery, and pronunciation of words produced by different speakers, voice recognition and encoding is extremely difficult. There are several audio output units available, consisting of prerecorded words or phrases stored on analog magnetic tape and called up by computer command. There are several programs in progress to develop "true" voice synthesizers capable of generating a large and flexible spoken vocabulary from a minimal set of stored information and programs.

Many data management systems with large quantities of textual materials use microphotographic techniques for the efficient storage of this data. Computer-controlled retrieval of this material is essential for its efficient use.

Film, as a storage medium, has large capability (50 to 1 over magnetic tape, for example). The ultimate limit of data compression becomes a matter of the nature of optical systems and the wavelength of light and techniques of developing the image rather than of the storage medium itself. Although 10- or 20-to-1 ratios have been traditional, Kodak used a reduction ratio of 60 to 1 in its minicard system, and AVCO has utilized ratios of 140 to 1. Others have experimented with ratios of over 1,000 to 1. The FMA File-Search equipment, as an example, used 35-millimeter film, a reduction ratio of 25 to 1, which permits 32 legal size pages to be stored on each foot of film, or 32,000 pages on one film reel. Retrieval, however, is limited to 56 characters per film frame, and these characters are separately applied—they are not part of the micro-filmed image.

PERIPHERAL DEVICE SELECTION

For data management system designers, this question must sooner or later be answered: "Which peripheral devices should I select?" Before even beginning to answer this question, several others should be answered.

1. What is the purpose of this system?

2. Who are the users?

3. What are the present methods of operation? (Flow charts should be made of present operations, with time, manpower, and materials allocated at each step, and a very thorough analysis of "why" it's done this way now and is it truly necessary!)

4. What is the cost of today's methods?

5. What is the potential growth?

6. What are the I/O message rates, quantities, and forms?

7. What is the size of the common data base required? How often is it used? How often is it changed?

8. What is the potential cost savings? What additional benefits will automation bring? (Faster reaction times, access to previously unavailable data, a competitive advantage in customer service, etc.)

As you can see, we have asked many questions and have not even begun to talk about peripheral devices. As system concepts are developed, process flow charts for a base-line automated system can be prepared. This is where the designer begins to ask which specific tasks should be automated and which remain manual.

Now we can begin to ask questions about hardware.

1. What are user I/O rates? How long can the user wait for response to his queries?

2. How much total storage will be required?

3. What levels of priority will be needed? Should this be hardware or software controlled?

4. Will paging, indexing, multiple access be required?

5. What security measures must be taken? Again...hardware or software?

6. What redundancy or back-up will be required?

7. Does this have to be a "turn-key" operation or can it be developed gradually?

8. What reliability, maintainability are required? Acceptable?

9. How much money is available?

As you can see, we are just beginning to scratch the surface, and we haven't begun to get technical.

At this point hardware analysis should be started. Trade-offs between specialized hardware and generalized software, and generalized hardware and specialized software are made. Trade-offs between auxiliary storage access speeds and main memory size are made. The technical literature should be studied; surveys of possibly usable equipment made, advertisements read (with some skepticism), and alternate systems drawn up for study. Cost effectiveness as well as total cost must be considered (remember Grosch's law).

Whose equipment should be purchased? Having those "800 devices" to choose from can make this question difficult. Find out how much "free" software is provided and how much software is actually available for what cost. Like the housewife shopping for a new dishwasher, try to find a satisfied (or dissatisfied) customer. Invite the equipment manufacturers in to explain their equipment. They will be more than happy to add to your education. If there is no other way, hire a consultant!

As you have already guessed, there is no single formula for the very best peripheral equipment for your system; the most important general rule is: Do not forget the *purpose* of your system!

BIBLIOGRAPHY

ADAMS ASSOCIATES, *Computer Characteristics Quarterly.*

ADAMS ASSOCIATES, *The Computer Display Review.*

BECKER, J., and R. M. HAYES, *Information Storage and Retrieval.* New York: John Wiley & Sons, Inc., 1963.

BONN, T. H., "Mass Storage: A Broad Review," *PROC. IEEE* (December 1966), pp. 1861–69.

CRAVEN, J. S., "A Review of Electromechanical Mass Storage," *Datamation*, XII (July 1966), 22–28.

DALE, B., "Never Fail Audio Response System," *1966 PROC. SJCC*, pp. 277–84.

DAVIDSON, L., "A Pushbutton Telephone for Alphanumeric Input," *Datamation*, XII (April 1966), 27–30.

DERSCH, W. C., "Shoebox—A Voice Responsive Machine," *Datamation*, VIII, 6 (June 1962), pp. 47–50.

FEIDELMAN, L. A., "A Survey of the Character Recognition Field," *Datamation*, XII (February 1966), 45–52.

HOAGLAND, A. S., "Mass Storage Revisited," *AFIPS Conf. Proc.*, XXXI (1967), p. 255.

HOBBS, L. C., "Display Applications and Technology," *PROC. IEEE* (December 1966), pp. 1870–84.

HOBBS, L. C., "The Impact of Hardware in the 1970's," *Datamation*, XII, 3 (March 1966), 26–44.

LUXENBERG, H. R, and R. L. KUEHN, *Display Systems Engineering.* New York: McGraw-Hill Book Company, 1968.

NISENOFF, N., "Hardware for Information Processing Systems: Today and in the Future," *PROC. IEEE* (December 1966), pp. 1820–34.

PETERSEN, R., "Manual Input Devices," *Computer Design* (December 1965), pp. 28–40.

POOLE, H. J., *Fundamentals of Display Systems.* New York: Spartan Books, 1966.

SEITZ, H. A., "New Approaches to Direct Access Computer Files," Systems and Procedures Association, *Ideas for Management*, 1967.

SIMEK, J. G., and C. J. TUNIS, "Hand Printing Device for Computer Systems," *IEEE SPECTRUM*, IV, 7 (July 1967), p. 72.

SUGART, A. F., and Y. U. TONG, "IBM 2321 Data Cell Drive," *AFIPS Conf. Proc.*, XXVIII, Washington, D.C., Spartan, pp. 335–345.

TALLEY, D., "Automatic Plotting in the Third Generation," *Datamation*, XIII (July 1967), p. 22.

TIPPET, J. T., *et al.*, *Optical and Electro-Optical Information Processing.* Cambridge, Mass.: M.I.T. Press, 1965.

Government Policy Implications In
Data Management*

MANLEY R. IRWIN

Associate Professor
Whittemore School of Business and Economics
University of New Hampshire

1. INTRODUCTION

Viewed in the particular, the series of dockets now pending before the FCC may appear to be the typical backlog of adjudicatory proceedings associated with any regulatory body. Viewed in the aggregate, however, these issues imply much more. They suggest that the question of terminal devices, the alternatives open in the use of communication lines, and the packaging of data switching and processing are exposing our communications policy and practices to an unprecedented reevaluation. At the very least these questions are likely to be on the agenda for some time to come, and their outcome merits the continued attention of those vesting an interest in computer time sharing and remote data processing systems.

This paper will identify recent policy developments that bear on the parts that make up a communication system; namely, the question of options in the terminal market, alternatives to carrier-provided communication lines, and the regulatory status of computer systems that both process data and switch record messages.

*This study was funded by a grant from the Office of Naval Research. The views expressed are those of the author only.

2. THE ISSUES

I/O TERMINAL EQUIPMENT

A first question deals with the validity of the carriers' foreign attachment tariff. As background it is useful to note that the carriers have historically provided what they regard as a complete communication service. That service includes ownership and control of terminal equipment, switching offices, and communication lines. Under this policy the carriers do not sell equipment or lines; rather a service is leased to their public message subscribers—a practice that in effect constitutes a tie-in between lines and equipment. To a certain extent the carriers have relaxed prohibitions against customer-owned terminal devices and equipment on circuits leased on a private dedicated basis. Nevertheless, the banning of customer-owned equipment continues to be enforced on the public exchange telephone network, and noncarrier-owned equipment is termed a violation of the carriers' "foreign attachment" tariff.

Any policy has its pros and cons and the foreign attachment tariff is no exception. The carriers submit that control of lines and terminals cannot be divorced from their responsibility of providing quality service to the general public. If, for example, a customer owns terminal devices that prove defective or inadequate, the user is under no obligation to repair its equipment, thus degrading the entire telephone network. Inevitably the carriers bear the onus of poor performance despite the fact that the cause may be beyond their control. The user, moreover, is under no obligation to update, modify, or scrap his equipment once he assumes complete ownership. What is at stake in the "foreign attachment" rule then is nothing less than the integrity of the nation's telephone system, and to protect that network, the carriers contend thay must control at least the interfacing modem between business machines and their network.

The growing skepticism surrounding the foreign attachment tariff begins and ends with economic cost. Subscribers, particularly computer users, find themselves exploring the quality and price of many devices in the terminal hardware area, a search incidentally that has fallen into two patterns.

A first grants the carrier's systemic integrity argument and thus permits the carrier to own and lease both lines and terminal equipment. In return for this control, however, some contend that the carriers ought to purchase equipment on a competitive bid basis rather than through their integrated supply affiliates. The carriers have an answer to this suggestion. They contend that their in-house purchases are dictated by considerations of price and quality only and that only their own manufacturing affiliates have thus far been able to meet that test.

A second option is to permit customer ownership of terminal and related equipment while at the same time to insure that such ownership will not compromise the nation's communications system. This proposal assumes the establishment of some kind of "fuse" concept coupled with common interfacing standards and/or the possibility of equipment certification. Whatever the means, the end is clear: many users want to buy rather than lease equipment manufactured by carrier or other supply affiliates in order to eliminate monthly leasing charges—charges which rise concomitant with the addition of out-station terminals.

The merit of these suggestions aside, it is significant that the FCC has now pending two cases which bear on the foreign attachment tariff. The first, the Carterphone case, involves the use of an acoustic coupler that permits interconnection between a mobile radio system and the nation's telephone network. The carriers oppose interconnection on the grounds cited above, and the FCC staff has, in challenging the assumptions of foreign attachment (or interconnection), both recommended approval not only of the Carterphone device but of all equipment banned under the foreign attachment rule.

The FCC Computer Inquiry also touches the question of foreign attachments. Responses by computer manufacturers, equipment suppliers, and data users are surprisingly unanimous in demanding greater flexibility in the ownership and control of their terminal and station equipment. The position taken by computer manufacturers is predictable, since they manufacture these devices either here or abroad. What is surprising is the emphasis on equipment choice by users who have no manufacturing interest in such equipment.

These two cases, the Carterphone and the Computer Inquiry, merit the attention of the data user, for their determination will effect the use, choice, and cost on a variety of devices critical in the development of remote access data services. Indeed, as computer systems move to the time-sharing mode, terminal and related market may assume an important part of a system's over-all cost.

COMMUNICATION LINES

The question of communication lines, their application and their use, is a second policy issue that has erupted quite recently. The issues under this heading include the question of leasing facilities versus service, the sharing of communication lines, and the question of alternative communication facilities.

Service versus Facilities. As noted, the carriers have long established the policy of rendering a complete end-to-end communication service to the public at large. While the computer industry does not question the relevance of this policy to the telephone user in the past, there are some who seek not "service," but "pipe." We shall term this the facilities and service dispute.

Oddly enough, one form of the facilities versus service question erupted subsequent to the passage of the Communication Satellite Act of 1962. Comsat was conceived as a joint venture, wholesaling its circuits to the international common carriers who, in turn, were to make "service" available to the public. Despite Commissioner Minow's pleading to the contrary, the Act permitted "authorized users" to lease circuits directly from the satellite corporation, thus permitting a possible by-pass of the international carriers. The application by large users such as IBM for authorized user status put the issue before the FCC.

More recently, the Department of Defense requested authorized user status in seeking some 30 circuits to the Far East. In this case the bids submitted by the overseas carriers and Comsat varied considerably; $10,000 to $12,000 per circuit per month versus Comsat's $4,000 per circuit per month. Clearly cost was the prime motive behind the Department of Defense's authorized user bid.

In the earlier case the FCC ruled that facilities alone did not qualify customers as authorized users. In the latter case, the FCC precluded the Department of Defense from by-passing the overseas carriers. While it is true that the Commission succeeded in negotiating a composite rate of $7,000, these decisions tend to limit Comsat's role as competitor in the overseas market and tend to preserve the Comsat-carrier-customer relationship. These decisions may become particularly crucial as precedents when Comsat begins offering service within the continental United States.

The service versus facilities quandary is also identified with the application by a firm for a specialized common carrier license between St. Louis and Chicago. The firm, Microwave Communications Inc., does not intend to sell "service" in the conventional sense but rather seeks to make available its circuits to subscribers to use at their discretion. Although the large computer manufacturers have been discreetly silent on this question, some users—particularly educational institutions and time-sharing firms—have testified that they require the flexibility of MCI's offering.

The carriers oppose MCI's application on technical and economic grounds. They suggest that letting new entrants into the market threatens their pricing policy which averages high-cost routes with low-cost routes. The fear is, in short, that new firms will skim the high-profit cream, leaving the carriers with low-profit skimmed milk. Carried to its extreme, the carriers predict that rising costs will translate into rising communication charges for everyone.

On the other hand, some question the validity of the cream-skimming argument. Indeed, the FCC staff has observed that MCI is seeking to develop new submarkets largely unexploited by the existing telephone and telegraph utilities. The question, in short, is whether a static or dynamic view of the market is relevant in this case. Whatever the outcome of this particular docket, the service versus facilities issue continues to crop up, to the obvious interest of the computer user.

Line-Sharing. *Line-sharing*, or the ability of several subscribers to colease a voice channel, has also commanded the attention of the computer industry. Here again, large scale sharing of circuits is viewed with some trepidation by the carriers. Their concern is that line-sharing is tantamount to reselling communication facilities and borders on the creation of pseudo-common carriers or, bluntly stated, competitors. This is not to suggest that all sharing is banned. On the contrary, line-sharing is permitted in three instances; the so-called authorized user tariff, the TELPAK tariff, and two Western Union offerings, SICOM and INFOCOM.

The authorized user case must be distinguished from the Comsat situation mentioned above. Here users may buy and release circuits to entities who are judged to be in the same line of business as the carriers' customer. Once a firm's customers qualify under the authorized user definition, the firms may release carrier-provided circuits. For example, firms supplying computerized stock quotation services have customers who qualify as authorized users.

Another form of line-sharing is embodied in the TELPAK tariff. TELPAK is a broad-band offering ranging in progressive blocks of circuits from A to D (12-voice grade to 240) on a private line basis. Introduced to counter the threat of private microwave to communication systems, TELPAK has been engulfed in controversy right from the start. Sections of the tariff, in fact, have been subject to court appeal and review.

Sharing of TELPAK channels is restricted to government and regulated firms such as power, rail, pipeline, etc.—a provision geared to match the limited sharing provisions established by the FCC private microwave case in 1960. However, the tariff was challenged on grounds that it was noncompensatory or unprofitale and that sections of it were not justified by competition from private microwave. The courts have upheld these charges as they apply to TELPAKS A and B, (12- and 24-voice grade channels).

The cancellation of TELPAKS A and B has led users to lease larger size TELPAK packages. Inevitably some users have experienced excess capacity and have sought a broadening of TELPAK sharing provisions in order to cut communication costs. The issue now before the Commission is whether the TELPAK sharing provisions are unduly discriminatory.

Two recent offerings by the Western Union Telegraph Company also contain variations on the shared circuit theme. A first, called SICOM, is a private lease service to members of the stock market industry. The service contemplates the sharing of leased circuits together with the sharing of computer switching. A second tariff broadens the sharing of lines and switching to industry at large in a tariff called INFOCOM. The telegraph company submits that its SICOM service attempts to meet the needs of users who seek to cut communication cost through cooperative use. On the other hand, the tariff has become embroiled in controversy, not so much because it embraces shared lines and shared computers, but because some members of the computer industry fear it is but a prelude to carrier entry into tariffed data processing services. The Commission has approved both SICOM and INFOCOM tariffs on grounds that they are limited to communication services only.

Alternative Facilities. Facilities separate and apart from those owned by the carriers are bound to be a controversial matter; and thus the promoting of new carriers, the evolution of CATV systems, the application of private microwave, and the role of domestic satellite systems all are a third area of concern to the data user.

As noted, the MCI issue fits the first category. If the FCC permits firms like MCI to establish and exploit new submarkets, the Commission will probably be faced with firms seeking to build on the MCI precedent. If the carriers introduce price competition similar to TELPAK, there is some apprehension that the very process of market entry will be stifled. On the other hand, if carrier price cuts are denied, then it is conceivable that the least efficient firm will establish price floors below which the carriers cannot penetrate—a situation not unlike the rate-making dilemma in the transportation industry. Still others contend that, if entry does not take place, then by definition the application of new innovation and new markets is consigned for all time to the existing carriers. The desirability of encouraging new carriers will undoubtedly be explored in the months ahead.

The application of satellites to domestic communications also looms as a competitive substitute to carrier transmission facilities. On this score, the Commission is faced with two dockets; the first involves the use of satellites by regulated entities, and the second, the application of satellites by non-regulated or private entities. The two are of course interrelated.

Satellite technology for domestic use generally was soft pedalled during the Congressional debates that preceded the 1962 Act. The general notion was that heavy capital requirements ruled that satellites could evolve only through the formation of joint venture, government or private. Six years and three generations of satellite technology tend to question those assumptions. Indeed, the petition of the American Broadcasting Company for permission to operate its own private broadcast satellite on grounds of cutting its communications cost dramatizes the rate of change in the satellite art. ABC's petition precipitated the question of satellites' application within the continental United States.

The rest was easily predictable. The Ford Foundation argued that the fruits of satellite technology ought to be made available for educational television. Comsat countered by observing that its Congressional mandate extended to domestic as well as overseas service. The domestic common carriers not only challenged the cost savings put forth by the Ford Foundation but sponsored their own satellite plan for domestic use. Today both dockets, the carrier-owned and the privately-owned, are now pending before the Commission.

What some term a silent war is now brewing between CATV systems and the carrier industry. CATV began as an extension of TV signals to rural areas where television signals were nonexistent. Using Microwave and cable pick-ups CATV drops a broadband cable directly into the home. Relatively little attention was accorded CATV's in the 1950's. However, with the movement of people from rural areas to cities, the broadcasting industry viewed such entry with mixed feelings, particularly in light of the possibility of diluted advertising revenues. Recently the FCC, seeking to give UHF-TV a chance to grow, has ruled that the 100 top markets in the country are off-limits for CATV systems.

To the extent that CATV makes available some six to twenty television signals, CATV systems hold promise of offering a variety of services to the home—newspaper facsimile, stock market information, educational and data information—a potential that places them in competition with the domestic communication carrier industry. These issues, in addition to copyright payments and carrier pole line attachments policy, are now questions pending before the courts and the FCC.

DATA SWITCHING AND DATA COMMUNICATIONS

A third policy issue, relevant to the remote access systems, is the joint application of computer and communication systems. Firms in the unregulated sector as well as the communications industry can perform data processing and message switching activities. The application of computer information systems by such corporations as Westinghouse and Ford on an in-house basis is fairly well-known by now. Perhaps less well-known is the attempt by unregulated firms to offer the communications-EDP package on a commercial basis.

Indeed, the grafting of store-and-forward computer technology to a stock market real-time quotation system in many ways was instrumental in kicking off the present FCC Computer Inquiry. The firm attempting such an amalgamation found that it was denied circuits on grounds that such activities embraced enough communications so as to infringe upon the prerogatives of regulated carriers. On the other hand, we have noted that the filing of tariffs on shared computer switching and lines by regulated firms has caused no little anxiety to the computer industry.

Undoubtedly the toughest and hence the most controversial issue associated with the FCC's Computer Inquiry is the regulatory status of computer/communications services. The carriers contend that, if data processing and switching are contemplated by any firm, the FCC is obligated to extend its jurisdiction to those firms. Computer firms, on the other hand, are adamant that data processing be declared off-limits from regulation. With respect to carrier diversification into data processing, the computer industry cautiously bases such entry on the formation of separate corporate affiliates; or if offered by the carrier itself require accounting practices that eliminate competitive advantages over the data processing industry. All of this requires staff and it is doubtful that the computer industry will add its voice to expanding the FCC's budget.

At first sight the recommendation of a carrier affiliate appears somewhat radical. In fact, however, it meshes with the existing structure of the communications industry, namely the vertical tie-in between regulated parent and supply affiliate. Whether such a recommendation by the computer industry is accepted by the communication carriers and the FCC is obviously speculative. Suffice it to note that a firm straddling a regulatory line does pose profound regulatory problems and responsibilities. A supply affiliate that sells services to its parent as well as to firms in the competitive market may be tempted to inflate prices to the carrier. Treated as operating costs, the carrier may pass them forward to their subscribers. This possibility, whether realized or not, does give the carrier affiliate an element of leverage denied firms in the data processing industry. Perhaps it was this fear that prompted the Justice Department to recommend a ban on transactions between parent utilities and their data processing affiliates.

3. CONCLUSION

The FCC dockets cited above have more in common than the aura of controversy surrounding specific issues. Clearly the bond that unites these proceedings must be assigned to a technology that prefers to run rather than walk. Whether that technology has any bearing on terminal equipment, computer switching and processing, or new means of data transmission, the issue that continues to beset public policy is who will control that technology and to what uses it will be put.

Large Data Base Mobilized for Service

BERNARD PETERS

Computer Systems Analyst
National Security Agency
Fort George G. Meade, Maryland

The National Security Agency, at its installation in the Washington area, has found the need to operate with a large data base with multiple inquiry stations and continuous update. The data base is made up of multiple files. The information is used by many people and is made available to these people via a remote access system with multiple remote terminals. I will describe some of the system characteristics to illustrate the capabilities of the chosen approach.

The development of this system followed an experimental implementation of the same system. Hopefully, we took advantage of all we learned from the pilot system. We feel that we have implemented a useful and effective system. The experience has been reasonable, although with some intense pain. The system is on-line and utilizes more than 100 devices as remote access terminals.

The remote equipments are used by untrained users. The users are not untrained in the sense of raw high school recruits or Army draftees; they simply are not computer specialists, keypunch operators, or computer operators.

This system is operated in a multipurpose environment. The requirement for the information-retrieval portion, although significant, is not sufficient to warrant the establishment of a large scale system, solely for the purpose of retrieval, and it is necessary that the retrieval programs operate in a multipurpose environment, which consists of some large scale equipments that support computational and other functions.

The information-retrieval data base we are describing has the following characteristics: The files are large. The data base itself has approximately

200,000,000 characters. This is not a large data base compared to some, but it is sufficiently large to encompass major problems. It consists of approximately 75 files, each of which is a distinct entity and has no relationship to any other file.

The most important characteristic is that the data base is volatile. Each file, to qualify to be in this data base, must have an average change of 10 per cent a day. In some cases a file has changed 90 per cent each day for three consecutive days. Updating is a most important consideration in the design.

The files are not error free. Because of the high rate of change and certain characteristics of the information, it is not possible to guarantee error free data. The users are aware that any particular item of retrieval data may be in error and are prepared to cope with the errors. This produces a certain amount of freedom and frees the system from absolute "bit perfect" requirements. However, this must be used cautiously so that there is no degradation of the system as the result of sloppy programming.

The response required by the system must be quick, complete, and furnish only the pertinent items. Quick has its own definition for everyone. In this system the most common type of query will be answered in less than 15 minutes and hopefully in 3 minutes.

The response must be complete because the nature of the files is such that the user cannot discern whether a "no information" answer is accurate or not. Similarly, receiving 10 responses to a query with 20 actually available would not be discernible to the user because of the makeup and the volatile nature of the file. Therefore, the system design must be such as to guarantee that all the answers are complete.

The retrieval mechanism must yield only pertinent material. It is inappropriate to return an excess of material for several reasons. Stations are small, in many cases consisting of a model 35 Teletype or its equal. The user is not interested in doing the retrieval analysis. He really wants only what is pertinent.

For a number of reasons the users have a unique role in this retrieval system. The central programming organization is to furnish the operating system. However, the users do all updating of the data base. They program all queries, because only the users have an understanding of the data base, which constantly shifts in emphasis and can change in format. Because of the large number of files and the variances in format, it is quite impossible to train a centrally located programmer to give proper consideration to each of the formats or files.

The user programs his queries in a number of available languages. For very heavily used queries or for complex updating he might program in assembly language. He has available to him FORTRAN and ALGOL. For all languages there are subsidiary functions that permit him to make use of macros. There is available for one time or low-use queries a language called

TILE. TILE is essentially an interpreter in the sense that Report Program Generators are interpreters. Because of the variance in the programming characteristics of the users, it is necessary that there be some system restraints on them. The skills of the users vary from very good to very poor with a median well above mediocre.

A restriction the system enforces vigorously is that not more than 5 per cent of any file may be selected for subsequent delivery. Five per cent of a very large file, for delivery on a Teletype, is an extreme venture. It could consist of 40 hours of typeout, if permitted. The 5 per cent maximum lowers the probability that the system will glut its internal storage areas.

Output will not require more than 1,024 lines of output, which requires 2 hours of printout on a Teletype. It is not acceptable that the user take more than this. Certain mass prints of a file for publishing of a manual are permitted to exceed this volume. Mass printouts are scheduled for low-use time of the computer, in the early morning or other off periods.

There is a further restriction that the user's query may not consume more than 5 minutes of Central Processing Unit (CPU) time. The limitation of 5 minutes of CPU time was established principally for the other functions and programs on the equipment, such as the computational programs, and does not limit any of the retrieval functions.

The programmer who utilizes this system is required to obey all conventions of the system. This system has a software security system which is operative and provides multilevel security. Therefore, the programmer is required to operate within a certain set of restrictions and inside an established body of doctrine.

Regardless of the language used, the programmer operates through a set of macros that establish the search, using a specific search technique, which is illustrated in Fig. 1.

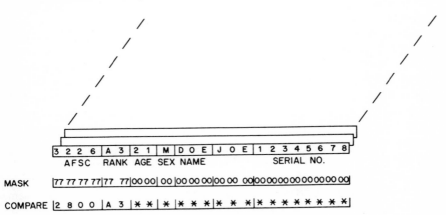

Fig. 1   Find all A3s with AFSC 2800

The search picks all items eventually, but it needs only one item at a time and passes the item through a mask. For instance, for the query, "Find all airmen third class (A3) with the Air Force specialty code 2800," we would search the query as follows: Read in the item and pass it through a mask of octal 7's as illustrated. Only the bits where there was a 1 bit are permitted to come through the mask. After the items have been pulled through the mask, the comparison is made for a complete match. If there is a bit difference, it is a failure in the search. If the item succeeds, there is a complete bit match, and the entire item, prior to the masking, is copied into a reserve pool for later collection and dissemination. This is essentially the search technique.

It is clear that this technique is too simple minded to work by itself. There are drivers on the front and rear of it. The driver on the front establishes the query from the language used by the individual making the query. It is not necessary for him to understand the mask and match requirement. He merely states what he wants to know, and the set up program translates this into a mask and a match capability. Similarly, the program sets appropriate flags on the mask and match that will lead to the calling of an analysis program to empty the pool of successful hits. This program, which runs after the search, performs the necessary derivation of the desired material. This program determines the format of the response and removes all material not germane to the particular question. In the example shown in Fig. 1 any qualified A3 is desired. If the search is for an A3 with Air Force specialty code 2800, female, to instruct a WAF station, we would search also on the sex fields.

The search technique is reduced to this simplicity to permit a generalized search against all the files of the data base. Every user that has a file in the system understands that this is the search technique and that he must live with it. There are some possible additions to the search technique. Instead of requiring an exact match, it is possible to compare an item to see if it is within a numeric range. Other simple modifications not requiring a perfect match but a near match are possible. Some of these considerations have been made available; however, they essentially are implemented in the summary program and are not part of the search.

For the medium for data, several alternatives were considered. The first was disks. Disks have several advantages. The common disk packs have a removable medium, direct access, and a high data rate. Some of the disadvantages are latency time and the severe updating problem. The volatility of the files make updating an extremely serious problem. It is necessary to avoid large scale update cycles. If one uses a random distribution technique for the information, the latency time for locating successive items to be searched is very difficult to overcome. If one overcomes latency by having the addressing scheme based on hash totals or a reasonable distribution system, then updating becomes very serious. At the time of design, the current high density disk packs were not available.

An alternative to consider for holding the data base would be a drum. The advantages of the drum are direct access, higher data rate, and simpler programming and updating. The update to a drum is simpler for a few items. It becomes simpler to program because it is simple to visualize. There is no arm positioning as in a disk. It has only rotary latency to consider for programming. The disadvantages of the drum are that the data is frozen to the medium. This can be very serious in the event of equipment failure. On a large scale drum, it might take as much as 3 hours to empty or reload should it be necessary to remove data.

The latency time of the rotation of the drum, as of the disk, is a serious problem. In a multiprogramming system the latency cannot be guaranteed. Updating is difficult for many items because of the latency. If a direct indexing scheme is used, then updating becomes difficult because of the complexity of maintaining the stability of the indexing scheme. The latency on a drum for the time of the next block averages 92 milliseconds. In a multiprogrammed machine, latency simply cannot be maintained because of the interrupts that will occur. On this particular system there are 50,000 interrupts in 7 minutes, and it would be impossible to predict the time between any two instructions not in interrupt lockout mode.

The medium chosen for this operating system was magnetic tapes. The latency on a magnetic tape for the time to the next block is 3.5 milliseconds. One might protest: "But you are required to take the records in a serial fashion." The response is: "We don't care what the order of the records is when searching for a particular item. We will compare all records."

What is the order of the records on the tape? The order of the records on the tape is whatever order is convenient for updating or any other reason. There is no particular reason to have an ordered set on the tape just so long as all records of a file are contigious.

In the pilot version of this retrieval operation as shown in Fig. 2 the tapes were searched in turn. The central processing unit selected each tape in turn via the standard I/O peripheral device. Searching in turn produced a search

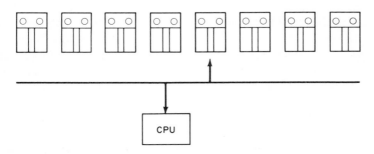

Fig. 2 Reference each drive in turn, maximum time to response 32 minutes

time of approximately 4 minutes per tape. This assumes 4 minutes to read each tape. The maximum time to response, for a number of reasons, was 32 minutes in the worst case. The average response was somewhat less but, in general, ranged between 10 and 15 minutes. This manner of operating was satisfactory for the pilot, which had 38,000,000 characters in it with approximately 15 files.

In order to improve the channel utilization and to capitalize on the possibilities of modern day equipment, a new channel scheme was developed. The new scheme used small computers and had one computer per tape drive. The small computers would search up to 40 items per pass. The utilization of small computers might seem a little extravagant. The computers involved were priced at approximately $30,000 for a 12K memory of 16 bit words.

The individual drive is controlled by one computer. The small computer absorbs all the failures, and the only transmissions to the central processor are for successful items. As in Fig. 3, each drive is searched by a small computer with only hits passing the main frame. Thus the maximum search time is 6 minutes for any item, regardless of when it arrives, without a special case limitation. This assumes 2 minutes for rewind and 4 minutes to read to the end of the magnetic tape.

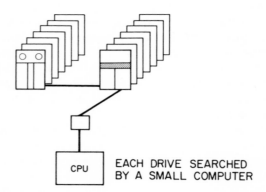

Fig. 3 Only hits pass to main frame, maximum search time 6 minutes

All the small computers are programmed in a similar fashion, and all hold exactly the same program. The search is parameterized to derive the hit. The hits are passed in blocks. Specifically, a hit is passed but once and is reported for all queries for which it has succeeded. The central processor arranges for multipass search. Depending upon the structure of the query, it is possible to have three, four, or five searches going on at once. All hits are entered into appropriate pools. Then the answer is derived from the study of the results in the pools. The simultaneous search by the small computer definitely increases the capability in a multipass search. In the pilot version, this multipass search was destructively slower.

One of the developments that became possible was on-line update of the magnetic tape. In the pilot version the updating was a serious objection to the process. It was necessary to store all updates in a drum pool. The pool was searched to complete a file search. As the age of the file increased and the number of updates rose, it became difficult to keep the search time for updates in the drum pool from exceeding the search time on magnetic tape. It was necessary to short cycle, update more often than once or twice a day, when the pool reached a certain level.

The use of the small computer made it possible to consider updating on-line. On the pilot system this was not acceptable because it was not possible to rewrite a tape. If all updates were stored on the drum for a volatile file, certain difficulties arose. Specifically, the collection of updates on the drum exceeded a reasonable ratio to the actual data on the magnetic tape. Excessive time was spent reading the drum. The solution to this was to short cycle. This delayed other actions and tied up the transfer system on the tapes. The small computers permit us to update the tape as we go, using character blocks of 20,000 and lengthened tape gaps. It is possible to rewrite any block on the tape within the constraints of the system. The strategy to update block B of blocks ABC is as follows: Read the block. Change it in core and make up the new image that is desired. Backspace over B, over A. This gives you a bench mark to condition the tape and position it. Read A short. The tape will now drift into the tape gap. Then write B. There is some jitter, but the experience is that this is successful.

Certain difficulties arise because there is no father-grandfather tape. It is necessary to exercise unusual discipline in how one handles certain errors. These errors can be bad if mishandled. The lengthened tape gaps reduce the tape capacity. The tapes are compatible. There is some trouble on inserts. Deletes waste tape.

There is noise in the gaps so there has to be a strategy for resolving noise in the tape handler routine. The operating executive was constructed by the systems programmers at this installation. They were not dependent upon the manufacturer to make modifications to the tape handling routines to get rid of the noise. The lengthened tape gaps definitely lower the number of rewrites of the full tapes. This reduces the damage that results from failure to transmit material.

In summary then, the information retrieval techniques used for this specific data base are based on:

1. a high change rate in the file

2. a general search of all items in the file without regard to order

3. a mask comparison of each individual item

4. a simultaneous search with multiple small computers

5. a scheme for permitting on-line update of magnetic tapes.

The retrieval operation is a portion of a dedicated remote access system. It is approximately 20 per cent of the remote access system and represents an economical, effective response to the requirements of the government.

Communications and Data Transmission

FRANK H. WESTERVELT

Associate Professor of Mechanical Engineering
University of Michigan

Data communications has become a new subject for the consideration of many "old-timers" in data processing. Increasingly often the pace of business, education, government, and military operations requires an exchange of data and programs with faster speeds and more direct interaction or response than is possible using computing systems without associated data communications.

Time sharing and the use of remote interactive consoles of many types have further sharpened this interest. More recent interest in networks of computers to provide ready access to diversified computing facilities specially designed for special types of computations, as well as to provide broad access to dynamically varying data bases and programs, has made a basic understanding of communications technology mandatory for computing system planners, managers, programmers, and last, but most important of all, users.

The Federal Communications Commission (FCC) has also recognized the peculiar importance of the interaction of computers and communications in the establishment of Docket No. 16979 in the matter of Regulatory and Policy Problems Presented by the Interdependence of Computer and Communications Services and Facilities. In reacting to this inquiry, data processing manufacturers and the communications common carriers have responded to safeguard their interests. The Association for Computing Machinery established an *ad hoc* Committee on Computers and Communications to respond helpfully to the Commission from a broad base of technical viewpoints. In the formation and implementation of the activities of this committee, it was found that the community of users is, in general, less well-organized, less well-informed, and probably more apathetic than the more specialized interest groups. It is the purpose of this paper to present an exceedingly brief tutorial on data communications and computers in the hope of developing some understanding of the problems involved in, and stimulating more interest and awareness in, this important subject area.

First of all, one must recognize that communications, in general, and data communications, in particular, may be carried by two broad classifications of services: private-line (leased line, point-to-point) and exchange (switched). These classifications are available from several communications carriers, including among the better known companies American Telephone and Telegraph Co., General Telephone and Electronics, and Western Union. Again, in general, the bandwidth or frequency response or information capacity of these services may be obtained in a range from less than 100 cycles or bits per second to about 10 megacycles per second. Finally, in general, private-line facilities permit the user the most carefully balanced communications channels and the greatest freedom of action in the use of those facilities but does not allow the flexibility of interconnection inherent in switched systems.

In other words, switched systems may be expected to be somewhat more "noisy" or error-prone but will operate satisfactorily at slightly lower speeds than available in private-line services. Switched systems, however, provide the flexibility of alternate routing and the ability to reach much more widely dispersed points easily. This flexibility may partially compensate for the additional usage restrictions normally imposed upon users of exchange facilities.

In addition to an awareness of these generalizations, the potential user of data communications facilities should become familiar with several terms or phrases closely related to the field. First of all, the process of transmitting information may take place in one direction only, called *simplex* transmission; in both directions but one at a time, called *half-duplex* transmission; or in both directions simultaneously, called *full-duplex*. The actual transmission may, in certain cases over relatively very short distances, be done by direct connection of electrical signals to a continuous electrical conductor. More typically, however, the signal is transmitted by one of various schemes of modulation using a pair of devices called data sets or modems (a contraction of modulator-demodulator). The data may be imposed upon a carrier waveform by varying the carrier frequency, called *frequency-shift keying*, or by shifting the carrier phase, called *phase-shift modulation*, or various other techniques. The data may be transmitted serially by bit or in parallel and may be treated either synchronously or asynchronously (using start-stop demarcation bit patterns).

The variety of data sets and devices available for data communication purposes may be appreciated by considering the following list of basic data set designations:

100's—Low speed [less than 300 bits per second (bps)] serial.

200's—Medium speed (more than 300 bps but within voice bandwidth or "voice-grade" service) serial.

300's—High speed (wideband) serial.

400's—Low and medium speed (voice band) parallel.

500's—High speed (wideband) parallel.

600's—Analog sets using voice bandwidth (and special modulation types).

700's—Wideband analog and special modulation types.

800's—Auxiliary data units; automatic calling, auxiliary signaling.

Of the above, probably the most familiar to users of exchange facilities are:

SERIAL ASYNCHRONOUS DATA SETS

103A1   A low speed (less than 300 bps) asynchronous full-duplex data set used normally on TWX services.

103A2   A data set similar to the 103A1 but used on DATAPHONE service in the normal telephone direct-dial exchange. Differs from the A1 by interchanging the frequencies used by the full-duplex device for originating and answering purposes.

202A   A higher speed (up to 1,200 bps) asynchronous data set capable of operating with voice-grade facilities. A 103 may not communicate with a 202 data set.

SERIAL SYNCHRONOUS DATA SETS

201A   A voice-grade (2,000 bps) half-duplex synchronous data set.

205A   A voice-grade synchronous data set employing four-wire service to achieve full-duplex operations.

In addition to the above, users of private-line facilities may employ a wide range of other data sets. The availability of "Touch-Tone" handsets has increased the use of the 400 series slow-speed parallel data sets for interaction with computing systems via audio-response units.

It is not possible in this brief space to provide a complete treatment of the subject of data communications. Therefore, the reader is directed to several references:

1. *Introduction to Data Communication.* Maynard, Mass: Digital Equipment Corporation, August 1967.

2. *Bell System Data Communications Technical Reference Manual,* American Telephone and Telegraph Co.

3. Eisenbies, J. L., "Conventions for Data Communications," *IBM Systems Journal*, VI, No. 4 (1967).

With this exceedingly terse introduction of some of the terminology of data communications it is now appropriate to turn to some of the problems encountered in the use of such facilities. Let us imagine that you are the manager of a large central computer system providing computing services as a utility to remote users via data communications facilities. If you may identify one or more very large, essentially full-period consumers of computing, you may elect to attach them through private-line facilities. However, the usual diversity of applications will probably minimize the number of such attachments. Thus you may move to provide switched or exchange facilities.

It is already apparent that no universal data set exists: a 103 cannot connect to a 201, etc. But you may not solve your problem completely by installing an inventory of various data sets either. It is not possible at this moment (although work is going on) to allow automatic transfer of data calls from one type of data set to another, assuming that your computing system is able to discover "what are you" as well as "who are you."

This problem is even more serious, however. Let us ignore the need for higher speed data communications and consider the 103A2 data set on the Direct Distance Dial (DDD) network. It is clear that a 103A2 cannot connect to a 103A1 because of the inversion of originate and answer carrier frequencies, but surely any device that attaches to a 103A2 should communicate with any other device attached to another 103A2. You jest!

Ignoring the encoding problem for characters (EBCDIC, ASCII, PTTC, EIA, etc.), which cannot really be ignored, the manufacturers of terminal equipment have taken advantage of the asynchronous behavior of the 103A to transmit at a bewildering variety of frequencies.

110	bps	Teletype Model 33 and 35
134.5	bps	IBM 2741 and 1050
150	bps	Teletype Model 37

This does not exhaust the list but does point out the problem: A device operating at 110 bps, for example, will not perform correctly if attached to a computer transmitting at 150 bps, even though the data sets are identical and the voice-grade line is the same and might have been thought to provide a common interface medium.

In addition, some asynchronous devices operate with 11-bit frames (1 start bit, 8 code bits, including parity, and 2 stop bits), although others use 10-bit frames (1 start bit and 1 stop bit). Again, we ignore completely the existence of codes that are not eight level.

If you have obtained the impression that things are somewhat confused in data communications, you are correct. The problem always belongs to someone else!

The computer utility manager is faced with an impossible problem: either legislate uniformity among users and deny the advantages of certain terminals and technological advances or install many trunk-hunting sequences of communication lines, each dedicated to a particular type of terminal. It is to be stressed that each of the various communications lines will be identical as to grade of line and data set but that service will not be possible except for the particular device to which the line has been assigned. In other words, when all Teletype lines are full, new Teletype terminal callers will receive "busy" signals even though lines are available to handle IBM 1050's (or vice versa).

In spite of the lack of positive terminal type identification conventions to permit positive "what are you" determination, a special data communications interface called the Data Concentrator for the IBM System/360 Model 67 multiplex channel has been designed and built by the Concomp (Research in Conversational Computaton) Project at The University of Michigan. Sponsored by the Advanced Research Projects Agency of the Department of Defense, this device consists of a small PDP-8 computer equipped with a special interface to the IBM 2870 multiplex channel and a special multiplexor and scan control to address the data communications facilities. In addition, special data set interfaces have also been designed and built. The Data Concentrator supports Touch-Tone input, automatic calling units, and several different types of voice-grade data sets. At present, four 201A and eight 103A2 lines are supported. The 103A2 interface is designed to work with 202 data sets as well.

In operation the Data Concentrator will assign clock frequencies, framing, code conversion, and device support dynamically to any 103A2 line. Thus the device may configure itself automatically from all teletypes to all IBM terminals or any mix with only one incoming phone number or trunk-hunting sequence. The capacity may be expanded to approximately 56 low-speed lines, if desired.

This work will be reported further in other sources. Except for the PDP-8 the Data Concentrator was completely designed and constructed by graduate students in the research project using programs specially created to generate wire lists and numerically controlled wire-wrap machine instructions. This effort shows considerable promise of simplifying part of the present data communications confusion. In particular, the work of D. L. Mills, K. E. Burkhalter, D. E. Wood, J. DiGiuseppe must be acknowledged in this effort.

Further work is proceeding to allow automatic transferring of calls among the dissimilar data sets and to allow automatic calling units to be released upon completion of dialing and reassigned to new communications lines to achieve improved use factors for this equipment.

In conclusion, the present state of data communications is developing rapidly with many interacting and interrelated factors impinging upon both computers and communications. It is hoped that this brief treatment of this rather complex subject may have served to stimulate further interest and work in evolving new systems, policies, and regulations to permit orderly and effective growth in this important area.

General Purpose Systems: The MARK IV
File Management System

JOHN A. POSTLEY

Vice President, Advanced Information Systems Division
Informatics Inc., Sherman Oaks, California

Investments in the hardware and software segments of the computer market were approximately equal in 1960. While hardware expenditures are expected to grow five fold by 1970, investment in software is expected to increase over seven times in the same period. Coupled with the estimate by *Fortune* magazine of a deficit approaching 100,000 programmers, these statistics suggest a growing need for efficiency in software development.

When computers first emerged on the business scene, most programming was done in "assembly language." In the latter part of the last decade higher level languages, such as FORTRAN, COBOL, and ALGOL emerged as a means to simplify our programming tasks. During the present decade, several organizations have sought further to simplify and reduce the programming effort through the development of general purpose software applicable to a wide range of computer-based problems.

As the need for such software systems becomes increasingly apparent, and as our capability to produce them continues to grow, organizations throughout the world, and particularly in the United States, reflect a growing acceptance of the general purpose approach to implementing their computer applications. Work that required months of effort in assembly language and weeks of effort in a higher level language has now been done in days by employing a general purpose system; such evidence is very persuasive to practical businessmen everywhere.

While some organizations are developing systems employing selected general purpose concepts designed to meet their own particular needs, perhaps the more interesting trend is toward the development of general purpose systems for use by a great variety of industries in an almost unlimited number of applications. Such systems include INFOL, developed by CDC for its upper 3000 series of equipment [1]; GIS, under development by IBM for the larger 360 equipment using OS/360 [2]; IMRADS, experimentally developed by UNIVAC for 1108 [3]; and the MARK IV File Management System, developed by Informatics Inc. for System/360 equipment from Model 25 through Model 75 under OS or DOS. By virtue of this broad applicability, Mark IV is available to over 60 per cent of all users of computers oriented to data base (file) applications.

In use (at the time of writing) at over 20 installations throughout the world, MARK IV is illustrative of the general purpose concept. MARK IV seeks to reduce programming requirements for business applications through automatic operation in accordance with problem specifications checked off on special MARK IV forms. For straightforward problems in the MARK IV framework, the user requires only *one* such form to check his problem specifications. For more complex problems four different forms replace the single one used in the simpler cases.

EXAMPLE

An example, employing the MARK IV Information Request, will illustrate the simplicity of this system, which is the primary goal of the general purpose concept. In this example an entire problem is completely specified using a single form.

The problem may be described as follows: Search the personnel/payroll file and produce a salary survey. Select all personnel who have a salary of greater than $450.00 and who have been with the company since 1960. Sort the selected information by department, within department by group, and within group by salary; sort salary in descending order. Start a new page for each new department. For each group within department, produce a total salary and a count of the number of persons selected in the group; compute and print the maximum, minimum, and average salaries in the group. Whenever the department changes, produce a cumulative total of salaries. Print the report on $8\frac{1}{2}$-inch by 11-inch paper using the date on which it is run.

The completed MARK IV Information Request required to solve this problem is shown in Fig. 1.

The request name, SALSURVY, is entered in the box entitled Request Name. The word, TODAY, designates the report date. The $8\frac{1}{2}$-inch width and 11-inch height are indicated by the codes B on the form. To select the persons whose salaries are greater than $450.00 (a decimal constant) and whose hire dates are greater than or equal to 1960 (a character string), this informa-

MARK IV FILE MANAGEMENT SYSTEM®

informatics inc.®

INFORMATION REQUEST

PAGE ____ OF ____

DECK I.D. (73–80)

* REQUEST NAME (1–8): SALSURVY

I R (9 10)

REPORT DATE (11–16): TODAY

REQUESTORS NAME (17): I. V. MARK

TELEPHONE/EXT.: 360

DIVISION/DEPT. (44): 30

REPORT FORMAT

SUMMARY REPORT ONLY? (50)	VERTICAL SPACING (51)	FORMS CONTROL (52)	WIDTH OF PAGE (53)	HEIGHT OF PAGE (54)	LINE NUMBERS? (55)

RECORD SELECTION

9,10	SEQ. NO. 11–13	LOGIC LEVEL 14	CONNECTOR 15	FIELD NAME A 17–24	OPERATION 25,26	BLANK, C OR D 27	FIELD NAME B OR CONSTANT 28–48
PR				SALARY	GE	D	$450.00
PR			A	HIREYEAR	GE	C	60
PR							
PR							
PR							
PR							
PR							
PR							
PR							
PR							
PR							
PR							
PR							
PR							
PR							
PR							

REPORT SPECIFICATION

9,10	SEQ. NO. 11–13	NO. OF SPACES BEFORE COLUMN 14,15	FIELD NAME 17–24	SORT: SEQUENCE 27	SORT: DESC.? 28	BREAK: CONTROL 29	BREAK: SUBTITLE 30	SUMMARIES: TOTAL 31	CUM. 32	COUNT 33	MAX. 34	MIN. 35	AVG. 36
R1	20		GROUP	2		2							
R1	10		DEPT	1		1	P						
R1	30		SALARY	3	Y			2	1	2	2	2	2
R1	40		EMPNAME										
R1													
R1													
R1													
R1													
R1													
R1													
R1													
R1													
R1													
R1													
R1													
R1													

TITLE (9 10 11 13 14 … 72)

T1 001 SALARY SURVEY - BY GROUP WITHIN DEPARTMENT∇

*KEYPUNCHING NOTE: THIS NAME MUST APPEAR IN COLS 1-8 OF ALL CARDS PUNCHED FROM THIS FORM.

Fig. 1

tion is entered as shown in the RECORD SELECTION section of the form.

The columns to be included in the report are indicated under the heading Field Name in the REPORT SPECIFICATION section of the form. By entering a 1 under Sort Sequence opposite DEPT, the report is sorted by department. A P under Break Subtitle on the same line designates a new page for each department, on which the department number is used as a page subtitle rather than as a column heading. By entering a 2 under Sort Sequence opposite GROUP, the report is given a secondary sequence by group; a third order sort order sequence of the report is designated by a 3 in the Sort Sequence column opposite SALARY, with descending order by salary indicated by a Y. The title of the report is produced from the entry made in the bottom line of the form.

All the summaries required in this example can be produced automatically by MARK IV. Since they are all summaries of salary information, they are designated on the same Information Request form opposite SALARY. Referring again to Fig. 1, the 2 in the Total column designates a salary total for each organizational group; the 1 in the Cum. Column causes a cumulative total of salaries to be printed at the end of each department; and the 2s in the Count, Max., Min., and Avg. columns cause MARK IV to compute, identify, and print the number of persons in each group, and the maximum, minimum, and average salary in each group.

A portion of the results of this information request, as produced by MARK IV, is shown in Fig. 2. The date and page number, as well as the title, appear at the top of the page. The number of the applicable department, 101, appears as a subtitle. Three information columns are headed GROUP, SALARY, and NAME. The information requested for group 20 appears first, followed by information pertaining to group 21. On the last several lines of the report, summaries pertaining to Department 101 are shown.

It should be noted that the entire report shown in this example was formatted completely by MARK IV. No statements pertaining to the report other than those shown in the information requests of Fig. 1 were made by the user. By thus relieving the user of the need to be concerned about essentially data processing matters, MARK IV realizes the true application orientation so long the goal of software developers.

By replacing the single Information Request form of this example with the four forms mentioned previously, the MARK IV user has at his disposal the full power of the system. He can thereby, for example, handle five input streams simultaneously. He can add, to the extensive logical capability previously available, a complete computational capability suitable for almost all standard data processing applications. He can produce printed or machine readable output in almost any form, such as preprinted forms, labels, data dependent reports, and reformatted direct access, magnetic tape, and card files.

FEB. 31, 1984   PAGE 1

SALARY SURVEY - BY GROUP WITHIN DEPARTMENT

101

		GROUP	SALARY	NAME
		20	$1120.00	SIEGAL, M. C.
			805.00	SMITH, C. H.
			600.00	JONES, T. L.
			580.00	WILSON, W. C.
			535.00	KENT, L. F.
GROUP	TOTAL		$3640.00	
GROUP	COUNT		5	
GROUP	MAX.		$1120.00	
GROUP	MIN.		$535.00	
GROUP	AVG.		$728.00	
		21	$1250.00	TONAI, M. M.
			905.00	KEITHLEY, L. J.
			600.00	WILLIAMS, J. G.
			550.00	MARTIN, T. D.
			525.00	JENSON, J. J.
			480.00	LEE, F. C.
			475.00	YOKUM, L. A.
GROUP	TOTAL		$4785.00	
GROUP	COUNT		7	
GROUP	MAX.		$1250.00	
GROUP	MIN.		$475.00	
GROUP	AVG.		$683.57	
DEPT.	TOTAL		$8425.00	
DEPT.	CUM.		$8425.00	
DEPT.	COUNT		12	
DEPT.	MAX.		$1250.00	
DEPT.	MIN.		$475.00	
DEPT.	AVG.		$702.08	

Fig. 2

The application of MARK IV is not limited to the areas discussed above. The System also incorporates a powerful capability to create and maintain computer based files on direct access or magnetic tape equipment. Almost any existing card, tape, or direct access transaction format can be entered into MARK IV for this purpose. Files and transactions against these files are defined only once; these definitions are catalogued by MARK IV. Thereafter, all file creation and file maintenance is carried out automatically by the System whenever input data are encountered. By relieving the user entirely of this task (once it has initially been performed), MARK IV makes a significant contribution to the performance of a task vital in all data processing operations.

EFFECTIVENESS

After about 4 months of experience in using MARK IV in a great variety of industry applications and computing environments, some tentative conclusions about System effectiveness can now be drawn.

It is now evident that the degree of software skill required to use MARK IV in a normal manner is less than that required by the senior or systems programmer. With a reduction in programmer training requirements and a reduction of the need to communicate with programmers, the task of the system analyst is correspondingly reduced. And finally, since management can, through the use of MARK IV forms, express its needs in a manner directly interpretable by the System, its task is made more straightforward from an intellectual standpoint.

Even at this early stage of its use, the general purpose approach, as represented by MARK IV, appears to be applicable to a wide range of data processing tasks. On the average, it would seem that MARK IV is currently used in about 20 per cent of the total data processing tasks of its users. In a few cases MARK IV is used for over 90 per cent of these applications. It has been observed further that a definite increase in MARK IV usage occurs as experience in its use is acquired. Thus, it would seem that, while initial acceptance of the concept is good, subsequent acceptance, based on experience, is even better.

During the course of its use in this great variety of situations, the opportunity to compare MARK IV with other methods, with regard to pertinent elapsed times, has presented itself. Three kinds of times have been studied: time to implement the System (program, checkout, and documentation), time to compile the program, and time to run the program. While such comparisons do, of course, depend significantly on the applications involved, average figures for the examples studied are at least 10 to 1 in favor of MARK IV for implementaton. Time to compile and run the programs in MARK IV, as compared to comparable COBOL programs, are approximately equal. Additional experience in the use of the System should serve further to improve these comparisons in favor of MARK IV.

FUTURE GROWTH OF THE GENERAL PURPOSE CONCEPT

The concept of the general purpose software system, as represented by the MARK IV File Management System, is an important new direction in computer programming. The conceptual goal is to produce a system whereby most computer users need not be expert software technicians as well as experts in the applications they seek to implement. This goal has been achieved in hardware of almost every kind (e.g., automobiles, television, and machine tools, as well as computers themselves). It is of vital interest to the entire software community that this goal be achieved in this area as well.

MARK IV itself has achieved its present state of development over a period of 8 years and through experience gained with four previous systems. [4, 5] Systems embodying the same general purpose approach have been developed by other organizations and for other computers. Some of these are mentioned in the introduction to this paper and in the references attached to it.

Like those for any significant product, improvements and additions to MARK IV are continuously under development. New features extending its capability in new areas of interest to MARK IV users are available now or under development as the need arises. Initially implemented for 360 Models 25 through 75, the MARK IV concept is potentially applicable to any computer of comparable size and capability. Plans to extend the capability of MARK IV on 360 and to make similar systems available for other computers are themselves in a continuous state of expansion as we move toward a new era in computer applications: the era of the general purpose system.

REFERENCES

1. OLLE, T. W., "Information Oriented Languages, A Generalized Language for Information Retrieval Applications," Control Data Corporation, Palo Alto, Calif.

2. BRYANT, J. H., and PARLAN SEMPLE, JR., "GIS and File Management," Proceedings ACM National Meeting, 1966.

3. "IMRADS Preliminary Users Manual," UNIVAC Division of Sperry Rand Corporation, Philadelphia, Pa.

4. "POSTLEY, JOHN A., and T. DWIGHT BUETTELL, "Generalized Information Retrieval and Listing System," *Datamation*, VIII, No. 12 (December 1962), 22–25.

5. POSTLEY, JOHN A., "Specialized Computer Programs Aid Planning," *Mayor and Manager*, VII, No. 12 (December 1964), 23–24.

Structure and Organization of Very Large Data Bases

NOAH S. PRYWES

Associate Professor, The Moore School of Electrical Engineering
University of Pennsylvania

1. PROBLEMS WITH VERY LARGE DATA BASES

This paper is addressed to the problems of automation of *very large data bases*. Our concept of what is considered very large changes with the progress of the respective technology. However, a few examples of automated data bases would suffice to illustrate the magnitudes of interest here. The size of a data base may be characterized by the number of entities it concerns and the average number of retrieval *terms* that apply to information about each entity. For instance, the MEDLARS file of health science publication is projected to contain 1969 information of 1-million citations with approximately 50 retrieval terms for each citation. A far larger file is that of the U.S. Internal Revenue Service, which contains about 100-million income tax returns.

It is important to note at the outset how very large data bases differ from small and intermediate size data bases. The difference is seen to be primarily in three respects:

1. Very large data bases are justified only in very large systems, involving many users and functions with the ancillary large computer complexes and networks.

2. High efficiency in processing, storage, and retrieval is extremely important where very large quantities of data are processed, as inefficiency may account for very large and sometimes impractical processing times.

3. A hierarchy of levels of storage is generally employed with large data

bases. The price of storage space is generally inversely related to the access time. Therefore, for very large data bases the information accessed least frequently should be located in the least expensive, slowest memory devices, while more expensive and faster memories should be used for the high rate of access information.

In view of the nature of the distinctive features of very large data bases that have been enumerated, this paper is directed to those individuals concerned with the design of large systems. Users of such systems need not be concerned with the above problems, as the classes of functions provided to them need not change with the magnitude of the systems or the data bases.

The subject of this paper is far too broad for coverage here and selectivity of the material must be exercised. The structure and organization of data bases have been recently reviewed and generalized [1], and there is no need to repeat this material here. Therefore, three aspects of special over-all importance have been selected for discussion here:

1. The need for a single storage and retrieval subsystem in order to retain unity, simplicity, and control.

2. The need for an easily changeable data base organization to retain efficiency based on automatically dynamically monitored operational parameters.

3. The need for automatic classification for storage assignment, particularly for efficient retrieval by natural language descriptive terms.

Sections 2, 3, and 4 are concerned with the past three aspects respectively.

2. A UNIFIED STORAGE AND RETRIEVAL SUBSYSTEM

This section presents the arguments for a unified storage and retrieval subsystem as a means for a central control point for data management and information services. An overview of system operation is first presented and followed by discussion of system design methodology.

USERS, WORKER PROGRAMS, AND MESSENGER PROGRAMS

In an automated system environment many processes must proceed simultaneously. Control points must be provided to manage and protect the incoming information, the repository, and the computer system processing. The total design should retain unity and simplicity. The approach advocated here is that a single subsystem should handle file management, protect against loss, assure privacy and integrity of the information, as well as provide generalized storage and retrieval services. The simplicity is a requisite not just to avoid complexity in program operations and system maintenance but primarily to reduce core memory requirements by having a smaller program that resides continuously in the core memory.

Figure 1 provides a conceptual overview of the total system. At the left of the figure are terminals with which users in the library communicate queries to the system and obtain responses. A query is received by a processor, which also provides various aids to users in query composition. A set of programs are then brought into the core memory (from the files in mass storage) to perform the processing required by the query. In Fig. 1 these programs are illustrated by "workers" (in the memory) each of whom carries out his assigned processing. The workers utilize various components of the processing equipment, sometimes simultaneously and at other times in sequence, as instructed by the operating system (not shown in Fig. 1), which schedules the work load and assigns memory. In the course of the processing these workers will require information from, or provide information to, the repository. Depending on the need, each submits storage or retrieval requests to the storage and retrieval subsystem, which performs all the functions of a data manipulation system (including retaining copies as safety against loss due to malfunction) and also serves as the one point of control over the access to the repository. This is illustrated in Fig. 1 by "messengers" who have the authority to enter the repository and store or retrieve information as requested.

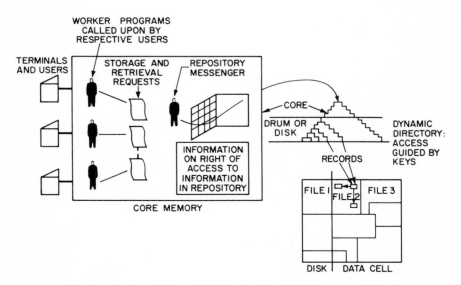

Fig. 1 Illustration of file system

In the design of the system a decision must be made about the division of labor between the two types of programs: worker programs and the storage and retrieval subsystem programs. The latter is designed to perform the basic storage and retrieval functions, sometimes quite complex but of a general purpose nature, i.e., independent of the specifics of the services required by the individual user. The worker programs have the function of combining a sequence of the basic storage and retrieval and other functions, so as to provide the specifically required services.

FILES

The repository is broken down several ways. First, the repository is divided into files. Each file is assigned a storage area in the mass storage devices and is accessed through an assigned portion of the dynamic directory. (The dynamic directory will be described below.) Files contain various data bases. In addition, private and semiprivate work-in-process files are assigned as working storage for individuals or groups concerned with updating the data bases. The total number of files in a large system is typically in the hundreds. The files are organized by a hierarchical relationship. There are the major files, which contain the directly useful information, and there are supporting inverted files, which contain index information about the respective major files. Files may be designated to contain such information as system management or use, programs, and various data respectively.

There are two reasons for the division of the total repository into files. First, this division facilitates the protection of privacy and integrity of the information. [2, 3] Users of the system will be assigned a right of access to the information contained in specific files. This is accomplished as follows: When a user begins communication with the computer system, he must first identify himself, and if required, authenticate his identification through response to specific questions submitted by the computer. The information concerning the right of access of the individual to specific files, as well as his identification, is retained in the users' file which is one of the system management files. It will be retrieved and retained by the storage and retrieval subsystem for the duration of any continuous interactive communication between the user and the computer system, viz., while the user is working at a terminal. In Fig. 1 this is illustrated by information about the user that is maintained at the entry to the repository for easy referral by the messenger.

Rights of access enforced are of six types:

1. to read the dynamic directory of a file,

2. to read the file,

3. to write in the file,

4. to block others from access to the file while it is being updated, and

5. to give other individuals permission to gain any of these accesses.

6. to establish a new file.

The usefulness of this approach may be illustrated by the following: A worker engaged in procurement activities will be entitled to change the information in the Inventory Item Procurement File. However, he will be permitted only read access to any information in the Master Inventory Item File, which is not concerned directly with procurement. This system also allows an individual to establish a file either for work in progress or for his own use, if he is so authorized. This latter feature is essential to the user of an on-line information system.

The second reason for dividing the information into files is to allow users to direct their queries to specific files for the duration of a particular phase in their work. [2, 3] This will eliminate a great deal of ambiguity. For instance, a worker engaged in procurement activity may specify that his queries should be directed to the Procurement File only. Thereafter, if his retrievals are based solely, for example, on some accession* number, then only the procurement information related to that number will be retrieved. Otherwise, total information on an item in which the worker has no interest would be retrieved from other files that contain information associated with the accession number. Thus, at any time he may specify that, until otherwise directed, all questions should be routed to the Procurement File only. He may at any time change this direction and query other files for which he has a right of access.

The user should be able to refer to one, several, or a class of files in a single statement to the system. For instance, the user may specify OPEN ALL FILES, which will direct queries to all the files that he is authorized to access. Alternatively, he may specify a class of files, such as OPEN ALL ITEM FILES, that will direct queries to the entire group of files (containing all kinds of information on library or inventory items, as the case may be).

RECORDS

Every file is divided into records. A record usually describes a certain entity. For example, in an Item File a record will contain all the information concerning an item. Another file will be constituted that will deal with the publisher or vendor (as the case may be) for the items. In the latter file a record will specify all the items originating from a certain publisher or vendor.

There is also a division of a record into elements. An element consists of

---

*Examples of accession numbers are found in a library file (for a document) or in an inventory file (for an item). An accession number is here a unique code assigned to each record that enters the system.

one or several fields of information as specified by a user. Where the records or the elements are of variable length, each such record in a file contains a "table of contents" that lists the elements included in the record and their (relative) starting addresses. For fixed format files this table of contents may be per file instead of per record. When a record is retrieved, the specific elements may be found and extracted by reference to the table of contents included in each record. The division of a record into elements may be specified or altered by the authorized manager of a file at any time. (This, in fact, is the means for file reorganization described above.) The detailed formats of records in a file will be stored in a record in the Files File for quick reference and ease of change.

RECORDING OF OPERATIONAL STATISTICS

The storage and retrieval subsystem is eminently qualified by its position as a central control point to engage also in the collection and storage of operating statistics.

The statistics to be collected are necessary to allow evaluation of the operation of each component and the total system. They serve as a form of feedback for continuous adaptiveness of the system to changing demand. The purpose of the statistics is also to assure improvements in efficiency requisite to obtain economic feasibility of new automated services. There are several types of statistics that will need to be collected.

One type of statistic is concerned with the usage of specific records—the tallies of usage being part of the respective records. At the time of the retrieval the storage and retrieval subsystem may restore the record, increasing the tally by one, thus maintaining a tally of usage of the respective records.

Another type of recording that is more encompassing is associated with maintaining tallies of usage of files. The tallies may be broken down by the basic function performed by the storage and retrieval subsystem—such as storage, retrieval, modification, addition, deletion, etc. It may also be broken down by the type of term that has been used for retrieval to the dynamic directory—such as author, journal-volume-issue-page, etc. The tallies may be stored in a record for the respective file in the File or Files. The process of maintaining a tally is initiated when a user "opens" a file. The storage and retrieval subsystem then maintains a tally for the specific file until the file is "closed" by the user. At that time the tally would be added to the tally of past usage in the record of the respective file.

Still another type of recording is associated with the users of the system. There is a record for each user in the users file. The storage and retrieval subsystem may monitor the operation of the user starting from the time that he identifies himself to the system when he initiates requesting services. The statistics for a user may contain the files that he opened, a tally of the basic storage and retrieval subsystem functions that were utilized in response to his queries, the period and times of usage, the storage capacity of his private files; therefore, the usage of the system by each user may be determined and checked against the alloted usage.

The recording activities outlined above illustrate the parameters that are critical to the efficiency of the entire system.

3. A CHANGEABLE FILE ORGANIZATION

The demands on the storage and retrieval subsystem vary greatly. The user becomes aware of this as a result of examining the monitored operational parameters as described in Sec. 2. Section 3 describes how this information can be used to increase system efficiency. Three technologies spanning the operational range of parameters are described.

PARAMETERS AND CONSIDERATIONS FOR SELECTING AN OPTIMAL FILE ORGANIZATION

File organization, often regarded as a theoretical subject, has in fact great practical implications here. The organization of the information in the automated repository has a major impact on the utility and efficiency of the electronic and mechanical devices and on the computer programs.

The theoretical and practical explorations of file organization in automated systems over the past decade have produced a number of techniques worthwhile considering. However, certain parameters derived from the natural breakdown or the use of the information bear a major impact on the utility and efficiency of the respective techniques. Such parameters may also indicate a preference of one technique over another in certain situations. The information about such operational parameters is not available a priori. It can be derived to some extent from simulation studies, but to a much greater extent it can only be derived from operational experience. In fact, it should be of the greatest importance in the design and implementation of a system to have an easily adjustable system that can readily be adapted to changing demands. Only in this way would it be possible to assure that the system would not become "locked-in" at an undesirable position requiring major corrections and reworking of the system.

Each function provided by the system has some cost associated with it. This cost consists of two factors—the required storage capacity and the processing time in accessing the information. The total cost of a function may be computed from these two factors. It is multiplied by the frequency of use of the function to obtain total cost. This then is the basis for economic feasibility of the services. It is, therefore, important to have a changeable file organization where these two factors can be varied to optimize the cost for services rendered. The system should utilize a variety of mass memory devices and storage and retrieval techniques that allow changing the cost of a function over a wide range to adapt it to the changing rate of usage. This adaptivity is requisite to obtain on-line rapid response services to the users at a reasonable cost.

For instance, four storage and retrieval techniques considered here are:

> Multilist
> Hash-Coding
> Inverted Files
> Automatic Classification

(These are described further below.)

Depending on the function, these techniques can be applied with widely varying speeds and costs, using for instance one or a combination of the following storage media:

> Core
> Drum or fixed head disk
> Disk with moving heads
> Magnetic strips

The operational parameters of the system and data base must be monitored. Among the parameters under consideration are the following:

> Number and types of retrieval terms*
> Distributions of frequency of use of terms
> Selectivity (or uniqueness) of retrieval terms
> Number of *significant* bytes required to express a retrieval term
> Number of random accessions required to retrieve from various parts
>   and types of the mass memory
> Number of simultaneous users
> Required storage capacities for various parts of the data bases.

Such parameters must be continuously and automatically monitored by the system itself. This information would be provided to the managers of the system, who will be able, after appropriate evaluation of various operational, economical, and priority factors, to change the presetting of the programs that organize the information. After the parameters have been changed, the

*A retrieval term means here any word, code, or name used singly or in combination in a retrieval query.

monitoring will continue, and the managers will be able to further verify whether expected improvements in fact materialized.

For instance, frequently used retrieval functions that utilize important, unique terms (each term referring to at most one record) or highly selective terms (each term referring to at most very few records) would justify using the expensive but very rapid dynamic directory methodology described below (section on "Dynamic Directory"). For less frequently used or less selective retrieval terms the inverted file technique is preferred. This is described in the section on "Retrieval by Widely Used Terms: Use of Inverted Files." For retrieval by natural language terms or phrases the automatic classification technique, as will be shown in Sec. 4, provides significant gains over competitive techniques. These techniques are reviewed below.

The selection of a device and a retrieval technique may be specified in a record format for a respective file. By changing the entries in the format, speed and cost of storage and retrieval in a file may be varied to be optimized for a certain frequency of demands of related services based on that file. By designating the accessing method (such as the dynamic directory, inverted files, or automatic classification) for each type of term in a record format the manager in fact selects the speed and cost of retrieval for each type of accessing of information.

DYNAMIC DIRECTORY

Retrieval through the dynamic directory is the fastest and most expensive method. To utilize this mode of retrieval, the manager may specify the elements (consisting of alphanumeric words, codes, or numbers) that are utilized frequently and that provide highly selective retrieval of records. The information selected will be referred to in the following as *keys*. This will generally include all fields in a record frequently used for retrieval. Each of the words, numbers, or codes designated as keys will always be included in the dynamic directory portion of the respective file together with an address of the respective record.

If there are several records containing the same key, the file manager may specify one of two options. In one option, all the records with the same key would be threaded by a list; viz., one record will contain the address of the next record having the same key, and so on, until all the records have been threaded. The address of the first record in the threaded list will be included with the key in the dynamic directory. This is the *Multilist* method of organizing information. The Multilist methodology has the advantage that it allows the associating of records in numerous ways through having a record contain the addresses of other records associated with it in a number of ways. It also facilitates the hierarchical structuring of the information. [4] The size of the dynamic directory is also reduced. The dynamic directory is usually stored in faster access, more expensive storage media than that required for records in the file. The keys must, however, be so selected that there are at most only a few records on each one of the lists, and a retrieval by a key in the dynamic directory is highly selective. For instance, in an item file in a library the following are envisioned as keys: the accession number, author's name, and an alphanumeric code that provides a combined identification of the journal, the volume and issue numbers, and finally, the starting page number of the article cited. Such fields of information in the record format are selected for keys in the belief that they would form the dominantly used means of access to the item records (accession by natural language descriptive terms and title words, also of major importance, is discussed below in Sec. 4).

The other option available to the authorized manager of a file is that of including in the dynamic directory the address of each record associated with each key. This avoids the need to thread these records by a list. This, in fact, is the *inverted file* methodology, which is advantageous when keys are less selective and access is frequently required by conjunction of keys.

The operation of the system is monitored frequently to identify the type of information used for selective accession of records, and accordingly, additional keys may be introduced or some of the initially suggested keys may be omitted.

As shown in Fig. 1, the worker programs are usually engaged in a sequence of storage and retrievals required to perform functions requested by a user. As they acquire or deposit information, the workers submit a storage and retrieval request to the storage and retrieval subsystem. The latter is illustrated in Fig. 1 by the messenger at the "gate" of the repository. The messenger performs only basic functions, general and applicable to all requests for storage and retrieval. He first verifies the right of access of the user to the information in the repository. If this is satisfactory, he then proceeds to make a reference to the dynamic directory, where he verifies that appropriate key (or keys for inverted file) specified in the query indeed exist(s) in the directory, and he obtains the address of associated record(s). The messenger then proceeds to the specified address in the specified file to retrieve or store the information. If additional information relating to the key exists in other records, a linking address is found in the first record (according to the first option described above) and the messenger follows the list until he has complied with the storage and retrieval request. The retrieved information is then submitted to the worker program requesting it.

In the interest of efficiency, the messenger (storage and retrieval subsystem) may order the accessing of records to minimize his work and the time required. Namely, once a reference is made to a certain track, strip, or magazine in a storage device, all other records being requested at that time "on the way" or in the "vicinity" would be retrieved as well.

Two methodologies are suggested for the dynamic directory by which a key is translated into an address. One is the Multilist tree [4], illustrated in

Fig. 1 by the triangular staircases. Illustratively, it may be compared to a multiplicity of forks in a road. The messenger, having the key extracted from the query, compares the key to the signs at each road junction and follows the appropriate signs until he reaches the terminal positions of the directory, where he finds the key and the associated addresses ordered in descending (or ascending) alphanumerical order. Thus a user may readily ask to be given the next "higher" key or the next "lower" key. He may ask for all the keys in a certain range or for the first or last key of certain type. This capability is considered of utmost importance in an interactive system, since generally a user does not have a knowledge of the specific spelling or codes of key words, but rather a generalized knowledge that requires he further select the appropriate keys when he is presented with the alternatives. For instance, a user may know only a few of the first letters of the name of the author with any assurance, and he may request information about authors' names in a certain alphabetic range whose citations are included in the system. A user may not be sure of the issue of a journal or the page on which the required citation is found; he may request information on citations in certain issues or through ranges of pages. He may ask for the latest issue of a particular journal. In all these instances, the specific key is not explicitly provided, but rather the area in the directory where the keys may be found and information about how to find the keys are provided.

An alternative technique to the Multilist tree is the hash-coding technique. [1] This technique is most efficient in translating known specified keys into respective addresses; however, it is not able to find the keys specified implicitly (as illustrated above) without a great deal of additional work and storage. If, however, it is found that the requirement for retrieval where the keys are not explicitly identified has been overestimated, a change should be made to the hash-coding technique and considerable gains in storage capacity and speed will be effected. This decision should be made in light of operational experience and should be based on the efficiency that will be automatically monitored and recorded by the system.

In summary, the file manager designates the keys for each file by identifying them in the record format. These keys then are the only means of direct access to records by the storage and retrieval subsystem—the messenger in Fig. 1. Accessing records by other information, not designated as keys, will require a sequence of accesses by the messenger as directed by the worker programs. An instance of such sequence of accessing is described in the next subsection.

RETRIEVAL BY WIDELY USED TERMS: USE OF INVERTED FILES

As indicated in the previous section, the dynamic directory contains only those terms that have been named *keys* used in queries at a high frequency and by which highly selective retrieval may be accomplished. There are a great many other terms which, in themselves, are far less selective and less frequently used. It is essential that (1) provision be made to store directories for these terms in less expensive devices and that (2) the updating requirements of such directories be reduced.

For instance, in a million item library there are ten to hundreds of thousands of citations in a specific language or published in a specific place of publication. If the query requires the counting or the retrieving of articles in a language or originating from a specific place of publication, in conjunction with requiring other more specific terms, the retrieval would proceed by looking up first the more specific terms in the dynamic directory, thereafter retrieving the respective citations, and finally checking whether the language or place of publication are those given in the query. However, it will also be necessary, although infrequently, to retrieve or to count items corresponding to a conjunction of, or a disjunction of, only the less selective terms. For instance, there may be a query requiring the count of the items in Russian published in England. It would be inefficient to include the terms Russian and England as keys in the dynamic directory, in view of the many records that would be threaded for each term or the many entries in the directory. In addition there will be the inherent expensive updating of addresses each time that records are rearranged in the storage devices. Therefore, separate inverted files are constituted where the terms and the reference (like accession number) to respective items that apply are stored. In fact, the retrieval time in some cases would be faster with the dynamic directory at far lesser cost.

To illustrate the use of these inverted files, consider a query requesting a count of all the items in Russian published in Great Britain. A worker program that performs retrieval and counting is called into the memory. This program communicates to the storage and retrieval subsystem (the messenger in Fig. 1) a sequence of retrieval requests. The first request is to retrieve a record in an Item Language File. Either Russian or its corresponding code will serve as the key in a record in that file. A look-up in the dynamic directory by the storage and retrieval subsystem will provide the address of the record. This record can be brought into core storage (one part at a time if the record is long). The record contains a list of all the *accession numbers* of the publications in Russian. A second query would be directed to the Item Place of Publication File. The key used here for retrieval could be one of several, such as Great Britain, England, or the corresponding code. This key will retrieve a record in the file containing all the *accession numbers* of publications in Great Britain. The intersection of the two lists will give the accession numbers of the items in Russian published in Great Britain. A count of these citations is then performed, producing the answer for the user. Alternately, the accession numbers could be printed out. Finally, if the user so desires, the retrieval of the item records may follow from the Item File.

This is performed by using as keys the accession numbers in the dynamic directory to get the addresses of the respective items. In a typical large library, the Language File may contain approximately 100 records, one for each language. The Place of Publication File may contain a similar number of records, one for each place of publication. The keys in respective records are the language, the place of publication, their synonyms, and the appropriate codes, by any of which the corresponding records may be retrieved.

When new item records are added to an item file, the corresponding accession numbers must be placed in the appropriate Language and Place of Publication Files records. Since these files do not contain addresses of the records, it is not necessary to update them when records are moved in storage. A judgment in fact has been made here that the retrieval by these keys alone will be relatively infrequent. During operation of the system the frequency of such queries will be monitored. This will then be one of the design parameters of the system. In examining these parameters, the manager of the system may decide whether the Inverted Files are to be placed in faster and higher cost, or in slower and less expensive, storage media; whether the information should be retained as Inverted Files or upgraded through entry to the dynamic directory; or whether these files should be altogether removed from the random access storage media. The change may be specified through use of the format record of the respective major file followed by a call in the programs that format the files.

4. RETRIEVAL BY NATURAL LANGUAGE TERMS OR PHRASES: USE OF AUTOMATIC CLASSIFICATION

RETRIEVAL BY NATURAL LANGUAGE TERMS

The retrieval in response to a query that consists of formulae or natural language terms or phrases poses a very special problem that cannot be solved efficiently by either the dynamic directory or the inverted file methodologies. The magnitude of this problem may be illustrated by the statistics in Tables 1 and 2. As indicated in the introduction to this paper, large automated data bases of 10^6 to 10^7 records (A in Table 1) are becoming a reality. In the input processing of these records or through usage, natural language terms are assigned to each record. These terms may be *descriptors*, index terms assigned from a schedule, or significant words derived from the title or assigned automatically to respective records. The number of such terms assigned to a record (B in Table 1) varies from system to system; however there are, characteristically, in the range of 10 to 100 terms assigned to a record. The number of terms in the vocabulary (C) also varies from application to application. An examination of existing thesauri would indicate that vocabu-

TABLE 1

MAGNITUDE OF PROBLEM OF RETRIEVAL BY NATURAL LANGUAGE TERMS

Number Of:

A = Item Records in File	10^6	to	10^7
B = Terms Assigned to an Item (av.)	10		10^2
C = Terms in Vocabulary	10^4		10^5
D = Average Number of Items Assigned to the Same Term $= \dfrac{A \times B}{C}$	10^3		10^4
E = Terms Specified in a Query (av.)	10		10^2
F = Items Referenced by Terms in a Query (av.) $= E \times D$	10^4		10^6

laries of between 10,000 and 100,000 terms are found in many systems. Finally, the simple formula shown in Table 1 for D provides a general idea of the average number of records that share a term. As shown in Table 1, D is typically a large number, 1,000 to 10,000. In fact, some terms may be assigned to a much larger number of records. This illustrates that these terms are not selective in that each applies to a large number of records. Retrieval by this type of term is, however, also required very frequently.

The retrieval using natural language terms may be based on a coordinate indexing approach. As indicated in Table 1, logical formulae constituting a query may involve 10 to 100 terms (E). These may be arranged in a number of disjunctive and conjunctive terms. The composition of such a query requires expert analysts knowledgeable about the content of the data base and the indexing system. To determine the records selected by a query, the computer needs to consider all the records referenced by each of the terms in the query and then to examine whether the disjunctive, conjunctive, or negation conditions apply to each record. As indicated in Table 1, 10,000 to 1,000,000 accession numbers of records would have to be brought into core memory for this processing.

Table 2 illustrates the high cost of storage and processing if the inverted file methodology is applied. The magnitude of the inverted file directory represents the additional cost of storage (in words). The number of words that must be transferred from secondary to primary storage may be considered as representative of cost of retrieval processing. As shown in Table 2, a very large directory of 10 million to 1 billion words (I) would be required, and a very large number of words (10,000 to 1,000,000) must be brought from the directory to the core storage where the processor would examine them to see if the logical conditions in the query formula are satisfied.

TABLE 2

MAGNITUDE OF DIRECTORY AND RETRIEVAL WITH INVERTED FILE
METHODOLOGY

Number Of:
Directory:

G = Records in Inverted File Directory; 1 Record Per Term = C	10^4	to	10^5
H = Accession Numbers Per Record in the Directory (av.) = D	10^3		10^4
I = Words in Directory = $G \times H$ (Assume 1 Computer Word Per Accession Number)	10^7		10^9
Retrieval:			
J = Inverted File Directory Words Brought from Secondary to Primary Storage = F (All Accession Numbers in Records That Correspond to Query Terms)	10^4		10^6

Considering the size of a directory (I) and the total time for transfer of accession numbers (J), we realize that on-line rapid retrieval (in seconds) with the present state of the art of equipment cannot be justified economically. In fact, a storage organization that will reduce these numbers by over an order of magnitude is needed.

Another difficulty, which arises, concerns the scarcity of highly trained analysts capable of composing effective queries and the length of time required to compose a query. Again, computer aids are required that will allow general users to address the system directly in the search for information.

AUTOMATIC CLASSIFICATION

The automatic classification method is of special importance in providing an efficient solution to probably the most knotty file design problem—that of retrieval in response to queries composed of descriptive natural language words or phrases. By application of this methodology, as will be illustrated, retrieval by such terms may be speeded by an order of magnitude when compared to using competitive techniques such as inverted files. Automatic classification also permits the use of cellular, slower, and far less expensive mass storage devices, such as the RCA RACE or IBM DATA CELL units.

The automatic classification technique has, however, another very important distinction; it places in close vicinity in the mass memory documents that are similarly indexed. This enables a user to benefit from an effect similar to browsing in material ordered according to subject on shelves in a library. Conventional browsing is a simple and direct retrieval methodology that should not be lost with the advance of automated data bases. The arrangement according to subject areas provides an alternative to coordinate indexing query formulation. Based on such arrangement, an interactive feedback retrieval scheme can be employed, involving automatic reformulation of queries.

The automatic generation of a classification system groups citations of documents in cells in the memory of the computer, very much as the documents on a common subject are grouped on respective library shelves. The retrieval process then consists of a search of several shelf areas in a large library to find the documents relating to a subject on which information is demanded.* A classification system, automatic or conventional, has then a dual purpose. It is a methodology for placing like documents together, but it is also a retrieval methodology by which one may be guided to the group of like documents that deal with his area of interest. Like conventional classifications, an automatic classification system may be used to put documents away but *only after* the classification system itself is derived from the documents. Namely, it does not precede the documents but follows them.

PARAMETERS OF AUTOMATIC CLASSIFICATION RECORD ARRANGEMENT

A file is arranged by automatic classification in cells, with a fixed number of records per cell, leaving some space for additions. The cell size, therefore, may be arbitrarily chosen to handle as many records as selected by the authorized manager of a file. Once he has selected the size of a cell, the automatic classification process will place the corresponding number of records in the cells, *attempting to minimize the number of different terms assigned to the records in the cell.* The number of the terms in a cell (M) depends on a number of parameters shown in Fig. 2 and Table 3.

The value of M is bounded by upper and lower limits as shown in Fig. 2. The number of terms per cell must equal, or be greater than, the number of terms in a single record in a cell. It must also equal or exceed the total number of terms divided by the number of cells. M also has an upper limit; it is less than, or equal to, either the number of terms in the total vocabulary or the number of terms per record multiplied by the number of records per cell,

---

*A cell search could be carried out in a serial manner or, if a cell is large enough, through a cell directory.

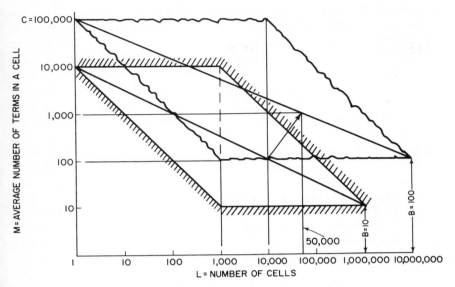

Fig. 2 Selection of number of cells

whichever is less. Thus the parallelograms in Fig. 2 indicate the area in which the value of M must be located for the two collections of records illustrated in Tables 1 through 3.

The scope of this paper does not permit a description of the process for automatically creating a classification system. Various methodologies have been used for this process. These consist of employing statistical techniques [5, 6, 7], computing distances between documents [7, 8], and employing co-occurrence of index terms. [9, 10] The last approach is simplest in terms of the complexity of the process and the amount of processing required. A collection composed of 4,000 documents with a vocabulary of 6,000 index terms has been processed to date. [10] Experiments are continuing at the University of Pennsylvania with collections of tens of thousands of documents. [11]

Experience to date [10] indicates that the number of terms in a cell (M) may be estimated to fall below a straight line on a log-log plot of Fig. 2. This estimate is also given in formula form in Table 3. Continued investigations currently underway will verify and improve this estimate. [11]

Another product of the automatic classification process is a directory where for each term are listed the corresponding cells. Illustration of directory size is also shown in Table 3.

The decision on the number or on the size of cells reflects trade off between two factors. The fewer cells there are, the smaller is the directory, as shown in Table 3. Also fewer entries from the directory must be brought into core memory for each demand search. On the other hand, the more cells there are, the smaller is the number of records in a cell, and the search of a cell is faster, and accessing a cell is more selective. Further investigation with reference to

TABLE 3

AN AUTOMATIC CLASSIFICATION CELL ARRANGEMENT

Number Of:
Directory:

K = Records in Automatic Classification Directory (1 Record Per Term) = C	10^4	to	10^5
L = Cells (Selection of Number of Cells Illustrated by Dots in Fig. 2)	10^4		5×10^4
M = Average Number of Terms Assigned to a Cell			
$\leq \dfrac{C}{L\left(\dfrac{\log C - \log B}{\log A}\right)}$	10^2		10^3
(see Fig. 2)			
N = Cells That Share a Term in Common (av.)			
$= \dfrac{L \times M}{C}$	10^2		5×10^2
O = Words in a Directory Record (av.) (One Word Per Cell to Which Respective Term Is Assigned) = N	10^2		5×10^2
P = Words in Directory = $K \times O$	10^6		5×10^7
Retrieval:			
Q = Cells References by a Term = N	10^2		5×10^2
R = Directory Words Brought from Secondary to Primary Storage = $Q \times E$	10^3		5×10^4

each system and its operational parameter is necessary to resolve the optimum trade-off values. However, to illustrate the operational improvements of this methodology, choices of 10,000 and 50,000 cells are indicated for the two sets of file parameters respectively. As a file grows ten fold (from 10^6 to 10^7 records) the number of cells increases five fold and the size of the cell doubles. Comparing the values of directory size P and words from directory transferred to primary storage R (Table 3) with the same parameters when using inverted file methodology I and J (Table 2) illustrates the possible order of magnitude improvement in retrieval efficiency.

INTERACTIVE QUERY REFORMULATING

On-line retrieval systems may be divided into two classes. The systems that aid user formulation of queries and retrieve respective documents are referred to here as *key-word systems*. The second type of system provides automatic reformulation of the query based on indications from the user of satisfaction or dissatisfaction with the retrieved material. In fact, in this manner the user guides and directs the search of the computer system.

An example of the key-word system is the BOLD system at System Development Corporation, developed by Borko. [12] BOLD utilizes on-line displays that assist the user both in acquiring a mastery of the system itself and in performing guided searches. The MULTILIST system at the University of Pennsylvania [13] is another example of a key-word retrieval capability based on list processing that facilitates split-second retrieval from large document collections.

BOLD and MULTILIST are representative of typical current systems. With these, systems retrieval is easier but the basic content of the query is not altered except at the insistence of the user. Thus, while formulation of the query is assisted by the system, there is no attempt at reformulation based on the results of previous searches, and the user is required to master the methodology of formulating queries.

The procedure in retrieval with a reformulating system may be as follows. A user may desire to search the collection to obtain a bibliography on a certain subject. He would then submit a query to the system consisting of a group of terms. These terms are first found in directories each with the respective cells. Then the system finds the cell or cells that correspond to the largest number of terms in the query. (Alternately, weights may be associated with the terms and cells selected that have documents indexed with the maximum total weight of the terms.) The user may then be shown a number of citations from the respective cell or cells, and he may indicate acceptance or rejection of certain citations as relevant or irrelevant. The terms corresponding to the accepted or rejected documents will then be examined by the computer, and the initial query may be reformulated. It will include additional terms derived from acceptable documents, or it will omit some of the initial terms that are in the rejected documents. Based on the newly reformulated query, a search is repeated, new cells are found, and their content is displayed to the user. This process may be repeated with the input from the user being primarily the approval or disapproval of retrieved material.

This approach has been experimented with in the SMART project, and the results have been evaluated to determine the effectiveness of this powerful strategy. [14] Experiments with this approach have been also conducted by Edwards. [15]

REFERENCES

1. LEFKOVITZ, D., "File Structures for On-Line Systems," ACM Professional Development Seminar, prepared for ACM by Computer Command and Control Company (Fall 1967).

2. PRYWES, N. S., and D. HSIAO, "A System to Manage An Information System," *Proceedings of the FID/IFIP Conference 1967 on Mechanized Information Storage, Retrieval and Dissemination*, Rome (June 1967).

3. HSIAO, D., "A File System for a Problem Solving Facility" (Ph.D. Dissertation, University of Pennsylvania, in process).

4. PRYWES, N. S., "Man-Computer Problem Solving With MULTILIST," *Proceedings of the IEEE*, LIV, 12 (December 1966), 1788–1801.

5. BORKO, H., "Research in Automatic Generation of Classification Systems," *AFIPS Conference Proceedings*, XV (1964), 529–35.

6. WILLIAMS, J. H., Jr., "A Discriminate Method for Automatically Classifying Documents," *AFIPS Conference Proceedings*, XIV (1963).

7. BAKER, FRANK B., "Information Retrieval Based Upon Latent Class Analysis," *Journal of the ACM*, IX, No. 4 (October 1962), 512–21.

8. NEEDHAM, R. M., "Automatic Classification in Linguistics," RAND Corporation Report, AD 644 961 (December 1966).

9. PRYWES, N. S., "Browsing in an Automated Library Through Remote Consoles," *Computer Augmentation of Human Reasoning*, ed. M. A. Sass and W. D. Wilkinson. N. Y.: Spartan Books, Inc., 1965, pp. 105–30.

10. LEFKOVITZ, D., and T. ANGELL, "Experiments in Automatic Classification," Report No. 85–104–6, Computer Command and Control Company (December 1966).

11. LITOFSKY, BARRY, "Utility of Automatic Classification Systems for Information Storage and Retrieval," Research in Progress, University of Pennsylvania.

12. BORKO, H., "Design of Information Systems and Services," *Annual Review of Information Science and Technology*, American Documentation Institute, Vol. 2, pp. 31–65. New York: John Wiley and Sons, 1967.

13. A collection of Physics Articles prepared by a project at the Massachusetts Institute of Technology under the direction of M. Kessler. The experiments conducted with this collection are a subject of a Master's Thesis, "Automatic Introduction of Information Into a Remote Access System: A Physics Library Catalog," by P. Gabrini at the Moore School of Electrical Engineering, Report No. 67–09 (University of Pennsylvania, 1966).

14. SALTON, G., Scientific Reports No. ISR–11 and No. ISR–12, Information Storage and Retrieval, Dept. of Computer Science, Cornell University (June 1966 and June 1967 respectively).

15. EDWARDS, J. S., "Adaptive Man-Machine Interaction in Information Retrieval" (Ph.D. Dissertation, University of Pennsylvania, 1967).